THE VITAL CHURCH

THE VITAL CHURCH

Teaching
Worship
Community
Service

Clark M. Williamson
Ronald J. Allen

Chalice Press
St. Louis, Missouri

Cover design: Vicky Nappier
Interior design: Elizabeth Wright
Art Direction: Elizabeth Wright

This book is printed on acid-free, recycled paper.

Visit Chalice Press on the World Wide Web at
www.chalicepress.com

10 9 8 7 6 5 4 3 2 1   98 99 00 01 02 03

Library of Congress Cataloging–in–Publication Data

Williamson, Clark M.
    The vital church: teaching, worship, community service / by Clark M. Williamson and Ronald J. Allen.
      p.   cm.
    ISBN 0-8272-4004-x
    1. Church renewal. I. Allen, Ronald J. (Ronald James), 1949– II. Title
BV600.2.W543   1998
253--DC21   98-25994
                                                                    CIP

Printed in the United States of America

Contents

Preface

This book is written for pastors and seminary students, many of whom are deeply involved in pastoral work in congregations during their seminary careers. It is very much *for* pastors and intended to provide support and insight for pastors struggling with the difficult problems facing congregations in a time when the general cultural attitude toward participating in communal activities and taking civic responsibility is in steep decline. It is for pastors of "mainline" congregations, the sort that have historically taken the greatest responsibility for the society in which we live and that have suffered the greatest losses since the 1950s and 1960s.

It is by two seminary professors who work together as colleagues. Each of us participates vigorously in a local congregation that is living in the midst of lean and struggling times. Whatever else might be wrong with this book, no one can accurately claim that we do not know what we are talking about when it comes to trying to revitalize struggling congregations. We have served as congregational elders, Sunday school teachers, and committee members. One of us is currently president of a congregation. We are intimately acquainted with the struggles of such congregations and, at the same time, with the richness of Christian life and the vitality of mission that they nonetheless exhibit.

Many pastors have helped us by discussing their congregations, describing and analyzing them, assessing their health, and helping us criticize and refine our ideas about congregational robustness. In order to set forth our case about congregational vitality, we tell some of their stories in chapter 6.

We express our thanks to those who consulted with us in the process of working on this book: Barbara Blaisdell, Bruce Roberts, Ross and Maris Walters, Bob Riester, Gay Reese, and Linda Patrick-Rosebrock. They are all talented, hard-working pastors, typical of those for whom this book is written.

This book is dedicated to pastors of churches everywhere who do the good work of shepherding God's sheep, those sheep who are sometimes faithful, sometimes wayward, but in spite of themselves, and by God's grace, the light of the world.

Introduction

Pastors are given and called to be "servants of the servants of God" (*servus servorum dei*). When churches ordain pastors, they place "the care of the churches" into the pastors' hands. The work to which those who engage in theological reflection are called is also that of being "servants of the servants of God." In this book, our hope is that we carry out this task faithfully. Theologians serve the church by serving the ends that the church is given and called to serve. The way we try to do that in this book is by articulating the self-understanding of the church that we find in its primary documents and suggesting that this self-understanding is as good a key to what is needed in a vital congregation as can be found.

We suggest that the church needs to look to the gospel of Jesus Christ, to what God gives and calls it to be, and to the scriptures in which it finds its self-description, in order to locate the sources of its vitality. Pastors seeking help in revitalizing congregations or turning them around from long periods of decline will find their greatest help in the most obvious of places: the Second Testament and the Christian tradition.

We are quite aware that we are telling pastors what they already know. We do this out of the confidence that the gospel is a word that bears repeating, not out of the belief that pastors are unfamiliar with it. Theologians frequently engage in redundancy, saying the same thing so often that we become boring. It is an occupational hazard faced by all who are servants of the servants of God. Our excuse, in this case, is the conviction that the New Testament description of an authentic congregation is also the description of one that is genuinely exciting and profoundly attractive.

If congregations are going to rediscover their vitality and halt their decline, changes are going to have to take place in how they understand themselves and how they go about doing their business. Here we briefly stipulate what some of these are. First, congregations must become proactive rather than reactive in their understanding of themselves and in their relation to their task and mission. A friend of ours began his career in the ministry in the 1950s. It was a time, he said, when one could go into a developing suburb, hammer a stick in the ground, put a sign with the name of the church on it, and people would gather. It was a "churchy" time in American life, an era characterized by what some neo-orthodox theologians at the time called, demeaningly, "temple-treading." Now we are tempted to look back upon it with nostalgia, because it was a time of large church buildings, filled sanctuaries, and Sunday school enrollments growing so fast that extensions of church buildings were being constructed all over the place.

Church life in the 1950s is not to be emulated. The churches of the 1950s do not provide a good model that we should imitate. Nor should we look back to that age longingly, as if it should set the standard for church life today. There is a serious spiritual yearning among many contemporary people; but we can be sure that, whatever they understand themselves to be looking for, it is not the stultifying conformity of the 1950s. The churches of the 1950s were full, to be sure; but they were also indifferent, unattuned to the movements of the spirit that were taking shape at that time. The most prominent feminists in American life were teenagers in the 1950s. The churches only slowly became hospitable to them and their concerns. Also, every major figure in the civil rights movement, including Martin Luther King, Jr., Malcolm X, and Cesar Chavez, began by protesting the shape of life in the 1950s. The culturally established churches of the 1950s have yet to respond adequately to this challenge.[1]

Today's church should bid farewell to the attitude on the part of churches and pastors that characterized that era. A vital congregation today must be mission-oriented, not maintenance-oriented. A vital congregation today cannot afford to have a pastor or pastoral staff that is merely reactive, willing to facilitate whatever others say needs to be done. Ministers cannot be void of ideas as to what ought to be done but need to be proactive, providing leadership rather than waiting for it to emerge.

Theologically this means that the church has to get clear about its identity as church and to proclaim and witness to that identity, in deeds interpreted by words and words fleshed out in deeds, in exciting and attractive ways, ways that at least hold forth the promise that they might attract people to it. The 1950s were the tag end of a long period of church establishment, of a time when being Protestant and being American were close to synonymous, although the insight was beginning to dawn that Catholics and Jews could also be American. The radical diversity of contemporary America, in which Hindus will soon outnumber Episcopalians, had not arrived.

Second, congregations will rediscover their authentically Christian vitality when they rediscover their authentically Christian identity and when they take steps to actualize that self-understanding in their life and mission. The church is a community of people called out from among the various peoples of the world by the Holy Spirit through the gospel of Jesus Christ. The church is that community given to understand itself, in any ultimate sense, in terms of and only in terms of its relation to the love of God made known to it in Jesus Christ. It understands itself as unconditionally loved by God and as called by God, in return to love God with all its self and its neighbors as itself. It is called to bear witness to this singularly good news and to do so never to its own glory but to the glory of God, the God of Israel and of Jesus Christ, and for the well-being of a hurting, estranged, sinful, and self-destructive world. It is called to actualize in its own life and to spread abroad in the world the love of God and the love of neighbor. It is called to constitute itself as church, as an authentic community of faith and love, unity and universality, and as such to be a sign to the world of an alternative to all those death-dealing ways of doing things that are indifferent to the well-being of our neighbors.

A church that works on constantly reminding itself of and teaching itself what this means and on seeking to embody it in its life and mission will, we think, find all the vitality it needs or can possibly stand. To this claim we should probably add some qualifying phrase such as "all other things being equal."

Vitality is not directly linked to the size of a congregation. We know vital communities that are small, medium-sized, and large. We also know small, medium, and large congregations that are effectively dead in their understanding of the gospel and in their life and witness.

There are some congregational situations that do not readily respond to the call and claim of the gospel. A former pastor whom we know recently commented that he left the ministry and took a secular job because he had concluded that being a minister in congregations that he knew was damaging his health and that of his family. Other pastors, who have struggled mightily to transform their congregations from being a collection of people who deal with each other in overtly hostile and belligerent ways, confess that their appreciation of the depth and virulence of sin and evil has grown immensely. There are pastoral strategies for trying to cope with intracongregational animosity and dissension, but such dysfunctional and self-defeating behavior proves remarkably resilient.

What should be done when a pastor faces this kind of situation in a congregation? One suggestion that we came up with in consultation with a pastor is to work intensely on a congregation's spirituality and to do this by way of encouraging intercessory prayer. Specifically, in the worship service all members should be requested to write on a piece of paper, an attendance card, or the worship bulletin the name of a person or family in an age group different from theirs. Then they should be instructed to do two things: to pray for that person or family and to go to that person or family and express their love for them in Christ. This is not a gimmick, and it cannot be a one-time effort. It is undeniably a Christian way to actualize what it means to say that we are all members of the body of Christ.

Our basic proposal is, first, that four factors are critical to the life of the church: its *kerygma* (preaching and worship), *didache* (teaching and learning), *koinonia* (the depth of its companionship), and *diakonia* (service to the needs of "the least of these").[2] Second we propose that a church is vital to the extent that these four factors are healthy in its life and mission. These aspects of the life of the church are described in abundance in the New Testament. Third, the quality and vitality of these four tend to rise or fall together. Fourth, while attention needs to be paid to all of them, it is to *didache*—the teaching of the Christian faith—that most mainline congregations have, over the decades, given the most benign neglect. We have noted in congregations that we have studied that the more intense they are as teaching/learning communities, the higher the quality of other aspects of their lives. Nor have we noted any exceptions.

Kerygma is the New Testament word for preaching. We use it in the somewhat broader sense of "presenting the gospel." Since we are always doing this again, we can also speak of it as "re-presenting the gospel." The gospel is re-presented to the congregation in the reading of scripture, in preaching, in the sacraments (where it is acted out, not merely announced). The sacraments of the Lord's supper and baptism are, in the helpful phrase of the Reformers, the word of God made visible, whereas preaching is an invisible, audible word. The gospel is also re-presented in prayer, in hymn singing, in the offertory, and in all aspects of the service of worship. In sum, *kerygma* refers to the preaching and worship of a congregation. In a healthy congregation these will be done well and thoughtfully, and they will be anything but boring.

II   *Didache* is a New Testament word for "teaching." Later we set aside a chapter to discuss why and how a congregation should become an intense community for teaching and learning the Christian faith, as we do for preaching and worship. Congregations that work hard at teaching the Christian faith also manifest a keen commitment to *diakonia*, service to the needs of a hurting world. The greater the involvement of a congregation in understanding the Christian faith, the less do different members and groups find themselves singing from different books when the time comes to make decisions about the church's life or mission. Education, which cannot be done solely by the pastor but cannot be done without the pastor's active involvement, is *how* the saints are equipped for their ministry.

We dare to suggest that the greater the understanding of the Christian faith in a congregation, the lower the level of conflict. Church conflict that we have seen, up close and personal, often stems from the fact that some members deal with every issue from a mind-set more informed by the culture or the world of business than from a sense of what the church is given and called to do. Others, operating from a different perspective, feel constantly defeated and drained of energy by the dominance of "the bottom line" and the way concerns over property dominate commitment to mission. We have listened for decades to the language used in board meetings and noted that the language of the Christian faith—its characteristic discourse—often shines by its absence. Absent the ability to talk the language of the Christian faith, the language of the world and its assumptions becomes the engine that runs the church.

III   *Koinonia* is one New Testament term used to refer to our common life in Christ, our life as members of one another. It includes but is not reducible to the warmth of "fellowship." *Koinonia* is the quality of community shared by those who love each other as they love themselves, who regard each other as equally important members of the body of Christ. Koinonia apart from *diakonia*—service to the needs of the hungry, the troubled, the lonely, the homeless, refugees from war—is indistinguishable from the animal warmth of the cocktail party at the country club. Koinonia apart from *didache*, teaching the Christian faith, is shapeless and likely sentimental. Koinonia apart from authentic *kerygma*, re-presentation of the gospel of God's love embodied in Jesus Christ, is idolatrous. Again, all four factors rise or fall together. In a spiritually robust congregation, they are all on the upswing. In a declining congregation, they are moving down. In an incoherent congregation, some are up and others are down, and they are inadequately related to each other.

IV   *Diakonia* expresses the church's commitment to feed the hungry, clothe the naked, house the homeless, and visit the sick, those in prison, widows, orphans, and the afflicted. A hearty congregation is significantly involved in the church's outreach (and thereby witness) to the world. It does this not because it thinks that the world will come rushing to its doors; it probably will not. It does not do it because it dreams that somehow it will manage to transform the death-dealing powers of the world into lovers of God and humanity. That assumption is the Christendom temptation, and we have flirted with it too long, whether we be fans of the emperor Constantine, right-wing Christian Coalition members, or liberal Democrats who look upon some politician as the next messiah.

No, the church feeds the hungry, clothes the naked, shelters the homeless, and works for justice for the simple reason that Jesus Christ has commanded us to do so. It is right to do this and wrong not to. It's that simple. The only proper response to the loving grace of God is to be graciously loving. The Christian ethic of gratitude lays a total claim upon us: not only shall we love God with all our selves, we shall love our neighbors as ourselves. When Jesus of Nazareth commanded us to do this, he did not think that Caesar would be grateful. But note: He could have talked to the poor and destitute about being the bread of the world until he was blue in the face, and they would have paid no attention. Instead he fed the hungry by the thousands and treated them as though they were indeed made in God's image. So he commands us. Oddly, in a congregation, the rule of Christian love works: the more we give away, squander, on the concrete needs of our neighbors, the richer our congregational life. A congregation that would find its life must first lose it.

These are tough times for churches, and many of their problems are not of the churches' own making. A strikingly low percentage of the population of contemporary North America is involved in any sort of public, communal, or civic activity. All the new communications technologies make it increasingly feasible for people to stay at home for work (commuting by computer), play (home entertainment from 135 channels), and even communication (the virtual community of cyberspace). "Burrowing" and "cocooning" are in; communal participation is out. Many voluntary organizations, not just churches, are seeing record drops in participation.

Yet we are bold to suggest that this is not the whole story. The only adequate philosophy of history, some wag once commented, is to say "this, too, shall pass." It will. Beyond that, we Christians think we know something about human beings, something given to us in the scriptures and in the tradition. Human beings are created by God for communion with God and one another; they are created for covenantal relation. Their hearts, as Augustine reminds us, have about them a restlessness that is an inbuilt striving for God. Augustine knew quite well from his own life that this ultimate striving can take some bizarre forms. But it is not finally satisfied until it comes home.

Human beings are the beings who need (whether or not they "want" it) to find authentic community and the meaning of life. That is good news because this is about all the church has to offer. So let us offer it faithfully, persistently, and as well as we can, and trust the rest to our Redeemer.

1

The Congregation:
Ideal Images, Harsh Realities,
and Exhilarating Visions

We ministers go into the service of the church, are willing to be ordained to the ministry of word and sacrament, because we are exhilarated at the prospect of serving a community called into being by the Holy Spirit through the gospel of Jesus Christ. Some of us grew up in the church, participated in Sunday school, and attended a seminary. Others came into the beloved community later in life through a variety of avenues. Perhaps we were looking for more meaning in life than our first careers offered. Perhaps we went through a crisis and found the church or a particular pastor or counselor to be of great help. In either case, our hearts were gladdened at the thought of serving this community that is the sign and instrument of the reign of God. We became steeped in the church's self-understanding that comes to voice in the scriptures and in the history of the church.

Ideal Images

We learned from studies in the Hebrew Bible that the people Israel in covenant with God, as Walter Brueggemann says, "embodied not only a theological novelty but also a social experiment as well." [1] The totalitarian, hierarchical social order of the surrounding city-states was rejected

9

and the Israelite order from Moses replaced it with a bold social experiment based on the claim that Israel's only identity came from allegiance to God. Its new order was socially egalitarian and politically decentralized, seeking to order society under God's intent (the reign of God, not some pharaoh) and to do so for the well-being of human beings. Covenant, says Brueggemann, is a "subversive paradigm."[2] About this, we can get excited.

Similarly, while studying the gospels, we learned that the rule of God into which Jesus invited "the lost sheep of the house of Israel" (Matthew 10:6) was a movement remarkably open to the poor, the hungry, and those who weep (Luke 6:20–21). Jesus' followers included not only the well-off but also a bunch of nobodies—the "children" or "little ones" of the time, the socially, politically and economically "humble." Jesus talked, shockingly, not just about a kingdom of the poor but of the destitute. "Destitute" (*ptochoi*) is the actual word Jesus uses in the sermon on the plain (Luke 6:20). His kingdom was not for the rich; the camel cannot get through the needle's eye (and there was no "needle gate"). With God, however, "all things are possible" (Mark 10:27). Even the rich can be converted, and in Acts, Luke tells the story of an oppressor (Saul) who became an apostle (Paul). It is a kingdom of weeds and undesirables (mustard is a weed and leaven is unclean), of the nobodies, beggars, the destitute, and it is here and now.

God's reign is "in your midst," given freely by God. We simply have to accept the gift and live on its terms and those of the future to which God calls us, and no longer on the terms of the Roman occupier. As a gift from God, it was a "brokerless kingdom," as John Dominic Crossan calls it, an egalitarian, inclusive community, a point that the gospels portray the apostles as having a hard time getting (Mark 9:33–37).[3] This community, that provided free and open eating and healing to hungry and outcast people, stands in continuity with the description of Israel as a people who understood themselves in terms of their relationship to God. Each community follows the "way of life" disclosed by God and is a clear alternative to the "way of death" practiced by surrounding empires, Egyptian or Roman.

This is the kind of stuff that gets pastors excited. Imagine a community living by God's will out of love for and service to a God whose redeeming and liberating grace brought them into being and calls them to be a "witness to the Gentiles" of this same redeeming, liberating love. Imagine an inclusive, egalitarian community that lives by service to "the least of these," those who need clothes, food, shelter, companionship, community. Such a community is indeed "the light of the world," the transforming "leaven in the lump" of humanity, the "salt of the earth" (Mark 9:50—salt; Luke 13:20–21—leaven; Matthew 5:14—light).

Or think of the local church with the major metaphor that Paul uses to describe it—the "body of Christ" in which each member, because a member of the same body, has some spiritual gift, some *charism*, to contribute to the community. The Holy Spirit has given each member some gift. Because *your* gift is the Spirit's *gift to you*, you take no credit for it but gladly share it with the community. This, too, is an egalitarian community in which no person is less important than any other because each one of the body's functions is indispensable to the health of the whole body (see Romans 12:4 and 1 Corinthians 12:4ff.). Although some members seem to have been set aside for specific functions, everybody engaged in some activity that expressed the spirit of the community and served its common life.

It was a nonhierarchical community. Ministry belonged to everybody in Paul's community. There were no church "offices" *as we know them*. Teachers did not teach because they were teachers, but were called "teachers" because they taught, "preachers" because they preached. Paul urged all members of the community to "teach, admonish, judge, comfort" (1 Thessalonians 5:14; Romans 15:14). He jettisoned the idea of ministry as practiced by a separate "caste." The congregation was the fundamental bearer of ministry.

This, too, thrills the hearts of pastors, and they try to actualize it in their congregations. Indeed, it excited the Reformers Luther and Calvin in their doctrine of the "priesthood of all believers" and their theology of ministry and church.

Imagine yourself as pastor in one of those congregations reflected in the pastoral epistles. The entire congregation would be concerned with teaching the Christian faith, developing a workable structure to carry out Christian mission, and focusing on pastoral care and the survival of the Christian community.

Or if you were a pastor in a congregation mirrored in Ephesians and Colossians, you would have a community that understood itself as the fullness of Christ's body, or as his lover. The congregation addressed by Luke and Acts combined these emphases, stressing the institutional as well as the charismatic. It cared deeply about the role of women and actively reached out to Samaritans and Gentiles, whom it welcomed. It was concerned to be open to the working of the Holy Spirit.

The congregation of John's gospel and letters paid little heed to questions of structure and inherited authority. Instead, it concentrated on the equality of all disciples living in community with God and Christ under the leading of the Spirit (the Paraclete). 1 Peter's community was shaped by Jewish symbolism (particularly that of the exodus). It thought of itself as the new Israel and the new people of God which, like biblical Israel, was a people "on the way." Or, the congregations reflected in Matthew and James held the *torah* in high regard. They sought to live out its commandments (which they understood as God's gracious gifts for the guidance of the Christian life) by practicing works of love on behalf of widows and orphans.

Wherever you might find yourself among these diverse congregations, in each case you would find standing out clearly faith in Jesus Christ, the practice of baptism and the Lord's supper, the apostolic preaching and teaching, a high regard for communal love, and an eager expectation of God's coming rule.[4]

Harsh Realities

Many ministers take up their vocations because they are profoundly attracted to some such vision of what the Christian community, by God's grace, is given and called to be. No congregation, however, is perfect. Nor are there any perfect pastors or professors. All congregations reflect what they are given and called to be in ambiguous and fragmentary ways. Further, we have to admit, sadly, that some are downright dysfunctional. Sometimes we find ourselves in congregations that grate on our hearts and minds, that conflict with everything we have come to believe about the church. Sometimes it seems that if an all-too-typical contemporary congregation were to place a want ad for a pastor, it would read something like this:

> Congregation long known for dysfunctional and self-destructive behavior, composed largely of cantankerous people who don't much like each other and won't like you either (with a few genuine saints thrown in for salt), seeks a pastor whom it can disabuse of his cherished assumptions about the church as a "beloved community." Salary for this position can be expected to decline over the years as the less thick-skinned depart the congregation.

That this congregation assumes the pastor will be a "he" is not accidental. It keeps busy making the life of its female co-pastor miserable. Perhaps the most difficult congregation that a pastor might be called to serve is one that has had a great history (or can remember times when it was much larger, which is not synonymous with having been great) but has since gone through a long period of decline. This congregation desperately needs leadership (as all congregations do) but finds ways to undermine every effort at providing it.

The following examples come from congregations known to the authors, with names omitted to protect the guilty (in the church we all live by grace and have to pray "forgive us our sins"). Seminary professors are sometimes reputed not to know or care much about the local church. This is not true of any seminary professors we know, and these stories are gathered from friends and colleagues who struggle to help the congregations of which they are members to learn how to live out faithfully the gospel of Jesus Christ.

1. One congregation has a high number of older members who are homebound or live in nursing homes. It is all the pastoral staff can do to visit them regularly, although a group of matriarchs in the church take some intermittent responsibility for this task. A retired minister, concerned with the needs of the elderly, volunteered to spend twenty hours a week calling on and organizing others to call upon these shut-in members. He asked to do this without being paid for it. The idea was to free up the time of the pastors so that they could help lead the congregation out of its long decline. Then some of the church's matriarchs, who thought of this activity as their private fiefdom, informed him that "we don't need you here." Eventually he left the congregation, and the elderly continued to receive the occasional attention of the matriarchs. Nor did the pastors gain the freedom they required to undertake the kind of strategic diagnosis, planning, and footwork that the congregation so desperately needs.

2. Another congregation, after months and months of educational efforts and discussion, started a new-style worship service (a "seeker's service") to try to attract some of the 55 percent of the surrounding population that is unchurched. The service met with some success, and its evangelistic potential was something in which one could hope. But the tone with which the board of trustees discussed it was entirely negative, consisting mainly of complaints that "we've never done this kind of thing before" and concentrating on how much it cost. Some members disclosed that they could think only as businesspeople concerned with the "bottom line." They asked: "Does the money collected in the offering at that service suffice to pay for it?" It did not occur to them to discuss the service in the language of the gospel of Jesus Christ or of the purpose of the church.

3. In yet another congregation, the personnel committee decided, upon hearing some complaints, to evaluate its pastors. They drew up an evaluation form inquiring into whether members thought the pastors spent enough time in the office, were available to meet whatever needs the members had, and exerted enough energy on the tasks of institutional maintenance, responsiveness to individual needs, and crisis intervention. The questionnaire asked nothing having to do with the purpose of the church and its ministry. Nor did it ask how well the pastors addressed the tasks that the search committee thought were critical to the well-being of the congregation when it invited them to be its ministers.

4. Another congregation showed in its regular board meetings an inability to discuss the business of the church in the language of the Christian faith. This is not entirely true. There was one member of this board who would regularly raise the question of what the mission of the church is, what Christ calls it to do. On one occasion it was discussing whether and on what terms to rent space to an African American congregation that was looking for more space in which to conduct its activities. When representatives of the African American congregation came into the board meeting they were alive and fervent about the gospel of Jesus Christ and their mission to troubled youths in the community. After they left, the board discussed the matter in the language of business, the law, insurance, and parking. One group of people looked, sounded, and acted like something that could be called "church." The other looked, sounded, and acted exactly like a secular landlord. One was spirited, the other spiritless. One wanted to serve Jesus Christ through a partnership with this congregation. The other was gratified for the rent that would ease its financial burden but concerned that it not lease its available, unused space too cheaply.

What we are trying to provide in this book is not a series of stratagems for intervening in these critical situations. That is like seeking out a mechanic in an out-of-the-way spot to replace the broken fan belt on the family car. What we are trying to offer is preventive maintenance. We are not asking what should be done about crises. We are asking: Why do these crises arise in the first place? We are convinced that a large part of them arise from a neglect by the church of one of its major tasks—that of teaching and interpreting the Christian faith in ways that are persuasive and exciting for members of the congregation. Most of the crises that we have noted in congregations can be said to stem largely from the inability of people to discuss their congregation, its dynamics and its mission, in the language of the Christian faith and/or from the lack of skill at putting into operation the practices of the Christian faith.

It Has Never Been Otherwise

The theologian Paul Tillich wisely reminded us that the actual church, concrete congregations such as "St. Peter's by the Mall," is *always* an ambiguous mixture of the essence of the church—what it is given and called to be—and its sociological actuality. The "paradoxical character" of the churches is made clear by the fact that each of them can be called "church" only if we add the phrase "in spite of" to the statement.[5] Each is a community of love, in spite of the bickering that takes place. Each is a community open to all sinners and egalitarian in its regard for them as "members of the body of Christ," in spite of the fact that some have more weight to throw around than others.

What makes it true to say that any Christian congregation is "church," in other words, is that the gospel of Jesus Christ is still witnessed to in the congregation, and it continues to take the risk of exposing itself to hearing that gospel. The churches insist, for example, that we study the Bible and learn from it. They may do this unaware that in doing so they place into our hands and plant in our hearts and minds images of what the church is given and called to be, images that will lead to dissatisfaction with and criticism of the church. But in making its own criticism possible and likely, the church is being faithful, again perhaps "in spite of" itself.

The church historian Robert Wilken argues that "There never was a Golden Age when the church was whole, perfect, pure—virginal. The faith was not purer, the Christians were not braver, the church was not one and undivided."[6]

And he is talking about the apostolic church, that earliest church that so many Christian movements like to think was pure. Never has it been the case that the church was unambiguous—and in this fact lies both our difficulty and our hope.

Let us look first at two New Testament examples of ambiguous churches and then return to the claim that in this ambiguity lies both our difficulty and our hope.

Paul and the Corinthians

Never has there been a more ambiguous congregation than the one Paul dealt with in Corinth. The Corinthians apparently jumped at the chance to interpret and live Christian faith as if this new message that they had encountered was simply another Hellenistic mystery cult. In many respects, the Corinthian congregation seems to have been a Hellenistic Gentile religious cult with an uncertain grasp on the gospel.[7] What kind of problems did this congregation present to Paul? For one, they were divided into blocs, each of which identified itself with the person who had baptized its members. They seemed to have thought of baptism as a kind of magic by which they shared the power of the person who had baptized them. They were "wise" and "spiritual" in contrast to other members of the congregation—religious snobs.

Some were involved in incest and other sexual offenses. Others were suing each other in pagan courts rather than settling their differences as Christians. Yet others had decided that the "freedom of the gospel" meant that "*all things are lawful.*" Their outrageous libertarianism convinced them that frequenting Corinth's brothels was quite acceptable. The members of the community who thought of themselves as "smarter" felt that they could eat meat offered to idols in spite of the fact that doing so might mislead their brothers and sisters. The richer members came to the Lord's supper and ate their fill while the poor went away hungry. Those who could not tell that there was much difference between worship of Christ and worship of Dionysius practiced a kind of incoherent spiritual babbling. And yet others were convinced that they were already resurrected and participants in the resurrection life.

How did Paul respond to the problems that surfaced in the life of this congregation? He replied to this problem–ridden congregation by teaching it the Christian faith. He reminded it of the meaning of baptism, the nature and point of the Lord's supper, the character of our care for one another as all members of the one body of Christ. To those members of different factions who felt themselves to be "spiritual" in ways superior to others and to possess "wisdom" as others did not, Paul proclaimed:

> But God chose what is foolish in the world to shame the wise;
> God chose what is weak in the world to shame the strong; God
> chose what is low and despised in the world, things that are not,
> to reduce to nothing things that are, so that no one might boast
> in the presence of God. He is the source of your life in Christ
> Jesus, who became for us wisdom from God . . . in order that, as it
> is written, "Let the one who boasts, boast in the Lord"
> (1 Corinthians 1:27–31).

He decided, so he said, "to know nothing among you except Jesus Christ and him crucified." His speech was not filled with "plausible words of wisdom, but with a demonstration of the Spirit and of power, so that your faith might rest not on human wisdom but on the power of God" (2:4–5).

He handled the case of incest as a matter of church discipline (imagine!). As to the matter of Christians suing one another in the courts of the Roman Empire, Paul comments that "to have lawsuits at all with one another is already a defeat for you. Why not rather be wronged?" (6:7). It is "already a defeat" because those who claim to be "members one of another" hereby show that they do not, in fact, understand themselves as so related to one another in bonds of love.

To the libertines who said "all things are lawful for me," he responded that "not all things are beneficial." Then he pointed out that there is a significant difference between whether something is lawful for me and whether I will allow myself to be "dominated" by it (6:12). Augustine would later argue that we get our loves distorted when we love things as though they were persons (ends to be served) and persons as though they were things (tools to be used). From Paul's perspective, the libertines who boasted of their "freedom" were enslaved to their bodies, whereas the truly "free" were those who did works of love in service to their neighbors: "Do not use your freedom as an opportunity for self-indulgence, but through love become slaves to one another. For the whole law is summed up in a single commandment, 'You shall love your neighbor as yourself'" (Galatians 5:13–14).

The super-smart disciples argued that they should be allowed to eat meat that had been sacrificed to idols because they knew, after all, that "'no idol in the world really exists' and that 'there is no God but one'" (1 Corinthians 8:4). Paul did not disagree with their theology but with their behavior, which was reckless and risked "destroying" those "weak believers for whom Christ died" (8:11). So he articulates a principle of Christian ethics: "'All things are lawful,' but not all things build up" (10:23, RSV). Whether something would "build up" or edify the community of the faithful was an ethical principle critically important to Paul.

At the Lord's supper, "each of you goes ahead with your own supper, and one goes hungry and another becomes drunk" (11:21). To them he teaches the Christian tradition: "I received from the Lord what I also handed on [*traditio* means "to hand on"] to you, that the Lord Jesus on the night when he was betrayed . . ." (11:23). And then he uses this account, our oldest, of the Lord's supper to do the job of practical theology. With it he addresses the community as to how it should celebrate the Lord's supper responsibly.

To those who boasted in their spiritual gifts, particularly that of speaking in tongues, Paul wrote his justifiably celebrated hymn to love in 1 Corinthians 13, beginning: "If I speak in the tongues of mortals and of angels, but do not have love, I am a noisy gong or a clanging cymbal." To those who thought that they already fully participated in the resurrection life, Paul points out that the resurrection is ahead of us; that many rulers, powers, and authorities have not yet been subjected to the reign of Christ; that we still have to die but that God "gives us the victory through our Lord Jesus Christ" (15:57).

In short, Paul's response to this ambiguous, cantankerous, divided, disagreeable bunch, who often gave voice to their feelings of superiority to one another, was to educate them more profoundly in the Christian faith. Their problem, as he saw it, was not that they failed to appreciate the importance of small groups in the church (they had quite a few of them). Nor was it that their congregation did not have sufficient visibility in the community. Given their behavior, it probably had all too much visibility in the community.

A pastor today can take Paul as an at least partially helpful example in dealing with a congregation. It would no doubt be better to take a gentler approach to the task than Paul did. Paul was not only outspoken and straightforward; he was frank and unreserved in his comments, and we do not know how successful he was in dealing with his congregations. Often he appeared highly frustrated. So we suggest that pastors put to use the skills they have learned as educators and counselors in the service of teaching the Christian faith.

The Boat in the Stormy Sea

The Synoptic Gospels tell the story of Jesus and the twelve crossing the Sea of Galilee during a storm. Whether this story is an actual incident from the time of Jesus with the apostles or reflects the situation of the church as it attempts to ride out the storms with which history afflicts it is not a choice that we need to make. There is no reason why it could not be both.

> On that day, when evening had come, he said to them, "Let us go across to the other side." And leaving the crowd behind, they took him with them in the boat, just as he was. Other boats were with him. A great windstorm arose, and the waves beat into the boat, so that the boat was already being swamped. But he was in the stern, asleep on the cushion; and they woke him up and said to him, "Teacher, do you not care that we are perishing?" He woke up and rebuked the wind, and said to the sea, "Peace! Be still!" Then the wind ceased, and there was a dead calm. He said to them, "Why are you afraid? Have you still no faith?" And they were filled with great awe and said to one another, "Who then is this, that even the wind and the sea obey him?" (Mark 4:35–41; cf. Matthew 8:23–27 and Luke 8:22–25)

Christians have long symbolized the church as a boat, as the "ark of salvation." The boat and ark serve as such symbols in the New Testament.[8] Not only Noah and his family, but the future of humanity and all the "living things" rode to salvation in Noah's ark. Little wonder that the church picked up and applied the symbol to itself. But just as Noah in the story had to ride out a flood, so the church has always found itself tossed about in the turmoil of history. The symbol of the World Council of Churches is that of a boat in rough waters. The church *always* sails on the choppy seas of history. No congregation *ever* has a completely smooth ride. We disciples *are prone* to panic and loss of faith. Yet the presence of God and Christ reassure us that we will not perish, the boat will not sink, and the waves will not overwhelm us.

Faith is the answer to fear and panic in this story (and in the New Testament more generally). The problem the church faces is a spiritual crisis. Only a spiritual response to it will be adequate. When the Gospels were written, the "storms" were probably persecutions. The disciples were tempted to succumb to the persecutions and in need of reassurance of the presence of the Lord to help them. The "storms" faced by churches in North America these days hardly compare to late first-century persecutions or, for that matter, to churches forced by authoritarian regimes to go underground if they are to keep alive an authentic Christian witness. Our problems doubtless owe more to the opposite tendencies: an unofficial establishment, ease with the commercialism and "everything's for sale" attitude of current American culture, and lack of any sense that involvement in the church is a radical alternative to what is involved in just being a good American. But for all that, our storm may be more threatening because immediately it looks less ominous.

Charlie Chaplin as a Model

Congregations today often resemble the disciples in that boat in Mark: panicked at the buffeting waves, bereft that God seems not to be present and certainly not solving our problems, and contributing to further and dangerous rocking of the boat by our faithlessness. Let us recall a delightful old, black-and-white silent film starring Charlie Chaplin, the great comedian. This film, *The Immigrant*, begins on a ship in the middle of the Atlantic. The ship is heading for Ellis Island with a boatload of immigrants and is plowing through heavy waters. It rocks about, back and forth, from left to right. People come staggering out of their cabins, lose their footing, slip, and bend over the rails, being sick at the stomach. It is hard to watch this scene without thinking of the church. That's exactly the way all too many of us are under similar circumstances.

But then Charlie Chaplin appears with his trademark hat and cane. A different response to the rocking of the boat is possible. Charlie Chaplin *dances to the rocking of the boat.* How is this possible? How is it possible, in a congregation in the midst of dire circumstances, that some folk can work constructively whereas others are prone to jump ship? How is it possible that some remain hopeful and oriented to the future while others grieve over a lost glory that is past? How is it possible that some try to keep alive the reality of Christian community when faultfinding is the preferred game?

Let us stay for a moment with this biblical image of the church as a ship in stormy waters. It is a biblical image, after all, and remarkably true to life. Anyone who has ever been on a ship on a trip across the ocean—as has one of the authors of this book—knows that there is a quite practical way to deal with rough waters and a rocking ship. It is simply this: Do not stay in a room with no window. Instead, spend time where you can see out, either through a porthole or on a deck with a view. Keep your eyes on the far horizon and get your sense of balance by watching it rather than the closer, moving walls.

Translating that into a more theological expression gives us this: We must keep our eyes not only on the immediate circumstances but also on the purposes of the church, the spreading in the world of the love of God and the love of the neighbor, the formation of a servant people, the needs of the vulnerable neighbor, and the loving grace of God that both empowers and commands us to attend to all things contained in the good news.

Since we cannot prevent the wind from billowing up the waves and making the boat rock, how can we learn and teach others to dance to the rocking of the boat? And how can we steer the boat to its destination, even though we will always have to do that in the face of the resistance that history and society and we ourselves place in our way? We can dance to the rocking of the boat if we are buoyed up by faith in the gracious presence of Christ with the church. We can be encouraged by all those saints in the past who made significant contributions to the church amid incredibly turbulent times.

Paul, Dietrich Bonhoeffer, and Martin Luther King, Jr. wrote profoundly Christian letters from their prison cells. Perpetua testified to her faith by her calmness in the arena where she would soon be martyred. Augustine produced profound theological and spiritual insights amid the collapse of an empire, a collapse for which some blamed the church. Reformers reshaped the church and brought it through in spite of efforts at military repression. We can dance to the rocking of the boat. Not without fear and anxiety, but by faith.

The church has always been ambiguous. Just as every Christian is at one and the same time justified and a sinner (*simul iustus et peccator*), so is every congregation. We should not be depressed by this fact but take hope in it. That we are justified reminds us of the redeeming presence of God and Christ with us, no matter how few in number we are, just as Christ was present with the panicked disciples on the Galilee and with the confused congregation in Corinth.

What is the Question?

In the current situation facing the so-called "mainstream" or "mainline" churches of North America, a search is going on for the "answer" to the plight of the churches. One immediate problem congregations face is that of declining numbers. Numbers decline for a wide variety of reasons, including population shifts, demographic changes, changes in the birth rate, socioeconomic changes in surrounding communities, generational shifts in aging patterns, and so forth. One reason for declining numbers, however, attracts our attention: the fact that significant numbers of people "dropout" of organized religion. People who list their religious affiliation as "none" constitute the fastest-growing category since the 1960s, as shown in sociological surveys.[9] As Loren B. Mead puts it, with regard to religious dropouts: "In the final analysis, the most important thing to do is to build strong, challenging communities of faith, communities that will stretch and empower congregational members. Where such communities exist, the need to drop out will not be felt."[10] The answer to a spiritual and theological problem must itself be spiritual and theological.

Paul and Mark were correct in posing spiritual, theological answers of faith to what were, in effect, not merely questions of, but crises with respect to, faith. A contemporary pastor who is committed to teaching the Christian faith, is clear about the purpose of the church, and goes about the task with some energy and enthusiasm can initiate renewal in almost any congregation. Nothing can substitute for the contagion of love that comes from being empowered by the grace of God.

The Problem

Mainline congregations tend to live on a now-dissipated cultural legacy from the past when they had become something of a "culture-religion," refusing to disturb middle-class values and unable to articulate a strong Christian vision of who we are and what God gives and calls us to do. We forgot to ask the question, What is it that the church can do that no other institution in the culture can be counted on to do? Mainline congregations have not held their own members over the past several decades because it has been too easy for those members to drift away from institutional religion altogether. Being closely identified with the mainstream culture means that people can drift off into that culture without the sense of having suffered any serious loss.

Among the current crop of books on the plight of the mainline churches, two writers (or sets of writers) in particular make this point. Both Kennon L. Callahan and the team of Stanley Hauerwas and William H. Willimon make comments that we would like to emphasize. Callahan stresses: "The day of the professional minister is over. The day of the missionary pastor has come."[11] The reason is that the "churched culture" of the 1940s has yielded to the "mission field of the 1980s" and afterward. Our culture now is better described as "unchurched."[12] Whereas in a churched culture people sought out the church, in the unchurched culture of our time "a substantial number of persons are not seeking out churches on their own initiative."[13] The church and the pastor are now required to be missional, both because this is what the situation demands and this is what being the church, with integrity, requires. By an "effective" church, Callahan means one that effectively enters into missionary outreach to people in an unchurched culture.

Similarly, Hauerwas and Willimon argue that we have definitively entered into a post-Constantinian, post-establishment time in the history of the church. The world in which we live "is no longer 'our world'—if it ever was." Few people any longer believe that any one "becomes Christian today by simply breathing the air and drinking the water in the generous, hospitable environment of Christendom America."[14]

We share with these authors this assumption: that ours is not, if it ever was, the age in which the church can duck the question of its theological identity by saying, as one early twentieth-century modernist did of Christianity: "It stands for the best in our civilization."[15] The assumption that our civilization and culture were permeated with the same message that the church is given and called to speak meant, for church leaders of that type and generation, that the church did not have to pay sufficient attention to its distinctive witness. Those days are gone, and the task of articulating its faith in a way that is appropriate to the gospel of Jesus Christ and adequate to the crises that we face is definitely before the church.

Biblical Models for the Church
Intense Teaching Communities

Of all the major periods of biblical history, only one compares to what we might call a "churched culture" or a Constantinian situation of establishment. That is the period of the Davidic monarchy. The other periods, for our purposes, are the pre-Davidic period of nonestablishment, the postexilic period, and the period of the early church.

Israelite religion during the period of the Davidic monarchy may be the biblical model on which Christians most often, unwittingly, rely.

Throughout most of Christian history, from the time of the Constantinian legitimation in the early fourth century until the recent realization that the era of establishment was over, this model served well the interests of an established, culturally authenticated Constantinian church. As biblical scholar Walter Brueggemann points out, this model had four features: (1) highly visible, legitimated, acceptable, and well-underwritten religious structures with endowments and acknowledged leadership, namely the temple and the priesthood; (2) public leadership in the office and person of the king committed to the same theology as the temple (in spite of the king's frequent violation of this same theology); (3) an intellectual leadership that was both civic bureaucracy and higher education lobby in the sages of the wisdom tradition—they supported the ideology of the temple-state; (4) witness of the prophets coterminous with the first three—the prophets expressed a purer vision of Israelite faith and criticized an establishment that would at least listen to them and sometimes hear them. The prophets were to some extent dependent on the very structures they so radically opposed.[16] This model, however serviceable it has been throughout Christian history, is no longer useful and perhaps should never have been acceptable.

Prior to this, as Brueggemann describes it, we find a different paradigm of the faith community. Its characteristics are more obviously pertinent to our situation. In it, (1) the life and faith of Israel were shaped by the exodus liturgy that called the power structures of the day (Pharaonic Egypt and the city-states of Canaan) radically into question; (2) the Sinai covenant and the process of interpretation of God's way of life that the Bible calls "torah" comprise a project in which Israel perpetually rethinks its faith and practice in the light of its liberation; this ongoing explication is the community of faith trying to discern the will of God; (3) this community had no solid organizations, no civic leadership and establishment, and no prophets. It had to extemporize. (4) Minus all visible props and securities, it relied on *telling its story often and well.*[17]

This intimates at least part of what might be a helpful model of the church in our, postestablishment, nonchurched time—a church that improvises, that is molded by its liberating liturgy of exodus/Sinai and crucifixion/resurrection, that keeps at the task of interpreting its scripture and its situation in relation to each other, and that sees to it that it both hears and tells its story well and frequently.

Another paradigm for the church is found at the other end of the Hebrew Bible, one that starts off in exile and continues in Second Temple Judaism. It has six traits:(1) The community exercised little leverage on public policy, being ruled over by the military leaders of successive empires; (2) it was enticed to blend into the enveloping culture and let its singular character vanish; (3) its principal duty was to preserve and refresh its language and forms of faith to insure its survival. It had three survival strategies: (4) it recovered its memory and rootedness to combat the tendency to forget its identity-conferring story and sink into the culture at large; (5) it developed a considerable practice of hope, filling its imagination with the discourse of the promises of God; (6) it became an acutely scriptural community. It formulated its scriptures, began to canonize them, interpreted them. It created the early forms of the synagogue, the place of the text and the "house of study" (*beth midrash*), and developed a new type of religious leader—the rabbi—who was teacher and custodian of the tradition.[18]

This is a good paradigm for the church in our post–culturally legitimated time when we can no longer rely on the·culture to tell our story for us. Instead, it is a time when human beings need some authentic alternative to the subhuman stories and images of human beings that the culture busily hawks. The church has to learn how to tell its story, teach its faith, use its language, and practice its faith if it is to survive as church.

All these same features stand out prominently in the life of the early church. Culturally it was anything but established and was often persecuted. It had no institutions and no buildings. Its leadership was charismatic but also filled with students of the faith who were, in turn, teachers. It paid attention to developing and telling its own story, writing its scriptures. It was intensely textual and incredibly creative. The fundamental bearer of its mission, ministry, and witness was the congregation. Prophets who imparted new revelations and teachers who transmitted and interpreted old ones were its most important leaders (other than apostles). It concentrated on telling its story, honing its skills to tell the story it lived by and to live by the story it told. It was not sufficiently culturally legitimate to provide prophets who could protest against the established power, who would not have listened to them in any case. It lived from and by the teaching of the gospel, as Paul makes clear both in his frequent citation of the role of teachers in the community and in his use of the letter as a way to carry out the teaching task.[19]

2

The Vocation of the Church:
Light of the World

In this chapter, we offer a way of thinking about the church and its mission that moves in the direction of helping the church think about appropriate Christian use of current approaches to church life and witness. The chapter calls attention to the essential nature and purpose of the church. It provides criteria by which to evaluate strategies for adapting the mission of the church to the ever-changing cultural landscape. It overviews a process for implementing innovative approaches to ministry, and outlines conditions necessary for change to take place in a local congregation.

We articulate a point of view that integrates the continuity of the church's purpose with the fact of continuously changing circumstances and the need for the church to reformulate its practices of witness in the light of such changes.[1] Such a Christian community can be a light in the world.

What is the Essential Nature and Purpose of the Church?

The essential nature and purpose of the church may be expressed quite straightforwardly.[2] The church is the community of human beings called into existence by God, through the Holy Spirit, to live from and by the gospel of God. The church witnesses to the grace and command of the gospel as the call and claim of the God of Israel offered to all the world and, hence, to the church, through Jesus Christ. It does so both to remind itself of what it is about, and, on behalf of the world, that the world might one day reflect the glory of God.[3] The church is both a recipient of the gospel and a sign of God's presence and purposes for the rest of the cosmic family.

The church is more than a collection, or even sum total, of individual Christians. The church is a community. This emphasis is evident from the call of Abraham and Sarah to become the parents of a mighty *nation,* through God's providential care for Israel, to the notion of the church as the *body* of Christ with its various members. God's purposes are inherently and thoroughly relational. Of course, God is concerned for individuals. God speaks through individuals (such as prophets) to the community. But God intends for the church to be a community whose very social identity is a witness to God's purpose for all things to live in right relationship with one another. In the language of biblical scholarship, the church is a corporate personality; each person represents the whole, and the whole is embodied in each person.[4] In the language of process philosophy, members of the church are internally related to God and to one another. In an internal relationship, each member is influenced by, and influences, every other member.[5]

The church witnesses to the gospel. The gospel (like the church) can be understood in many ways. The following is our understanding of the gospel, one that we believe can be widely accepted in the Christian community. The gospel of Jesus Christ is the good news that God graciously and freely loves all creation and everyone in it (oneself included), and that this God who loves all the creatures therefore demands justice for all. Jesus Christ reveals the gospel to the church. In this context, justice refers to being in right relationship. God wills for all elements of the created world to live in right relationship with one another. Those are relationships of mutuality, encouragement, and support. In short, God calls for the members of the world to live together in love.

The gospel is cosmic in scope. Of course, God loves people and wills justice for human communities. In addition, the gospel is for the squirrel running on the electric line outside my window, and the salamanders choking in toxic waste, and the snow-crowned Rocky Mountains, and the distant moons orbiting Jupiter. As human beings are learning through the environmental crisis, when we forget the cosmic scope of the gospel we not only shrink the focus of the gospel, we imperil the future of existence itself.

Further, the gospel is dipolar. It "(a) promises God's love to each of us as the only adequate ground of our life, and (b) demands justice from us toward all others whom God loves."[6] The stress on God's call for justice in this articulation of the gospel guards against cheap grace, while the stress on the unconditionality of divine love warns the church against the various forms of works-righteousness that still plague the Christian house.

The call of the church is to witness to the gospel. To be sure, as the definition of the church above notes, the Christian community needs to attend to its interior life. A church that does not nourish its life with the resources of the gospel will soon find itself impotent. However, the church does not exist for its own sake. *The only justification for the continuation of the church is its witness to the gospel of the living God.* The ecclesial witness takes place in both word and deed. Acts of witness in the Christian community run the spectrum from preaching, teaching, and public conversation to changing a baby's diaper in the nursery, greeting visitors at the door, and demonstrating on the town square for (or against) certain governmental policies.

The Bible suggests an image for such a church: light of the world.[7] Isaiah, whose community is in exile in Babylonia, says that God has given Israel "as a covenant to the people, a light to the nations" (42:6; cf. 49:6, 51:4). The Matthean Jesus tells the disciples, "You are the light of the world" (Matthew 5:14). Although light was a symbol with multiple dimensions of meaning in antiquity, our present purpose does not require an exhaustive study of the meanings of the symbolism of light.[8] It is enough for us to note that light was associated with the presence and knowledge of God, with bringing order to chaos, with justice in community, with providing illumination for life's journeys, with God's designs for the world, with God's eschatological purposes. God's light shines in the world in multiple ways.

Several things are noteworthy for our thinking about the church as a light in the world. The light is intended to help people see the world as it is. When our world is enshrouded, it is often difficult to distinguish true and false, right and wrong, acceptable and unacceptable, clear and ambiguous, certitude and relativity, and various degrees between. Light can help us see the landscape so that we can make such distinctions.

An analogy: Our children have all passed through a phase in which they were afraid to sleep in a dark room. The curtains stirred by the wind appeared to be ghosts. The shadow of a lamp looked like a monster. One of our children, hungry in the night, found what was supposed to be a candy bar hidden under the bed. It turned out to be a small stuffed animal. Not tasty. A night light—even the tiniest one—allows children to see what is actually in the room and to respond appropriately.

Some people perceive the world much like our children perceived their unlit bedrooms. People need a light to give them the perspective to name things and to relate to them appropriately. Just as the room is bigger than the candle, so the world is bigger than the community of the light; the light is intended to help the world. As light, the church is intended to help the world see things from the divine point of view and to model God's design for all.

To be sure, the life and witness of the church are not always bright and revelatory. The church can hide itself under a bushel basket, and even quench its own wick. Hence, we take solace in the fact that the church is not the only source by which God's light shines in the world. The biblical wisdom tradition, for instance, affirms that we can know God by reflecting on life experience. Many find the knowledge of God written in the face of nature. Since the Holy Spirit is omnipresent, it follows that the world can become conscious of the divine presence in any situation. God is never without witness in any time or place. However, the church is especially appointed to testify to the light of the gospel and its implications for our self-understanding and behavior.

The Church and Its Expressions

The gospel is universal in its message and scope. But the essence of the church is always expressed in a particular context. The church witnesses to the universal gospel in a discrete time and place. The church, then, has no choice but to make use of the elements of a given culture. The question is how, and to what ends, the church makes use of the possibilities offered by its particular setting in history in order to express its witness.

This situation has qualities that can be potentially positive and negative for the church's testimony. On the positive side, embodiment in the particularity of culture allows the church to make a witness that can be genuinely contemporary. The church, and those who receive its witness, can recognize what the gospel offers them and asks of them in the specific realities of their situation.

This understanding of the nature and purpose of the church does not tie the church to particular formats of ecclesial life that must be passed from one generation to another. The church is not only free to change its styles of life from one time and place to another but is obligated to ask whether such modifications might be desirable in order to help the witness of the church fit its different contexts.

At its best, *the church is in a relationship of mutual critical correlation between its witness and its situation.*[9] The church correlates its modes of thought in the issues with which it deals, as well as in its patterns of institutional expression, and its actions beyond the congregation. On the one hand, the church correlates its message and testimony with aspects of the prevailing culture; the church helps the church understand the gospel and its implications in the idiom and style of the contemporary setting. The church correlates the questions and needs (both recognized and unrecognized) of a particular moment in history with the resources of the gospel.

On the other hand, insights in the prevailing culture can cause the church to rethink its message and witness. The correlation needs to be genuinely mutual. A key term in this movement is "critical." At its best, the church does not simply accept the expressions, values, and practices of any contemporary culture as normative; the church criticizes those aspects of the culture that subvert or deny the gospel. The correlation is genuinely critical.

For example, the Gospel of Mark interprets the story of Jesus in an apocalyptic framework, evidently for the sake of a community with an apocalyptic worldview. John, by contrast, interprets the story of Jesus in the context of Hellenistic Jewish literature that is touched by Middle Platonism and that relies heavily on the transformed Jewish wisdom traditions represented by the Wisdom of Solomon and Ecclesiasticus. In the fourth century, the church embraced Greek philosophy in order to articulate the fullness of the doctrine of the trinity as we know it. These moves partake of mutual critical correlation. They helped make the witness of the church accessible to the communities in which it found itself. At the same time, these hermeneutical transpositions transformed aspects of the Christian message.

As a consequence of being embodied in the particularity of culture, the witness of the church is seldom pure. For instance, in the period of earliest Christian history, many congregations manifested inappropriate witnesses. In Corinth at the time of the apostle Paul, the community became divided to the extent that its division contradicted its essential unity in Christ. Some in the church apparently minimized the ongoing role of the cross in the formation of Christian identity and witness. Several church members engaged in promiscuous sexual behavior. The church's social relationships at the Lord's supper reflected the same oppressive social stratification as were present in the culture at large. Some Corinthians evidently denied the resurrection of the body. Indeed, the New Testament is a veritable library of missteps in witness that the various authors attempted to correct by writing the various documents that today comprise the New Testament.

In the process of mutual critical correlation from one setting or worldview to another, some things in Christian witness are always lost—and some gained. Furthermore, the church is itself a created entity and, therefore, is limited in its ability to manifest the Transcendent. Its witness is always partial and relative. And the church exists in a world in which sin is ever present and deceptively powerful; the perpetual presence of sin disfigures the life and witness of the church. Consequently, the testimony of the church is nearly always compromised in both word and deed.

We can see the ambiguities of the process of adaptation of ecclesial life to particular contexts by considering some examples of church architecture, worship rites, and polity in relationship to their moments in culture. At the very beginning of its life, when the church was a part of Judaism, it met in houses and its rites were very similar to the simple rites of the synagogue. Its leadership, in the form of elders, evidently functioned similarly to the elders in Judaism. As the church became mainstream in more Hellenistic and Roman settings, its buildings, rites, and organization assumed some of the characteristics of the dominant culture. The basilica and its rites are reminiscent of the temple, and they also echo the architecture and pageantry of state functions. Rome has its Caesar (and most subsequent states have their monarchs) and the church has its Bishop of Rome. In the 1800s, many church buildings in this country were built in the style of Federal architecture, a style often symbolizing democracy. Many churches were organized according to democratic rule. The approach to worship in many congregations of the Presbyterians, Baptists, Methodists, and Disciples (and other churches whose worship was not regulated by a prayer book or other liturgical guide) was much like the prevailing style of government and other forms of public life: simple, dignified, reserved, and orderly. Each of these moves helped the life of the gospel and the church become accessible to people who lived in its sphere of time and space.

Yet, as the church takes on characteristics of the prevailing culture, it is sometimes difficult for the distinctive calls of the gospel to be distinguished from the usual (and sometimes unloving and unjust) practices of the populace at large. It is sometimes difficult for a church to be prophetic in a culture when the church appears to be at one with the culture. Indeed, some people assume that the purpose of the church is to bless their culture and the culture's oppressive values and practices. Hence, the church needs to remember that its incarnation is always in a mutually critical relationship with its culture.

Consequently, the church ought to speak of the *relative* degree of faithfulness or unfaithfulness in its witness in a particular cultural setting. Preachers and congregations need always to determine the degree to which particular forms of witness conform to the criteria discussed in the next section of this chapter (appropriateness to the gospel, intelligibility, and moral plausibility). The church can then seek to reinforce points at which Christian testimony seems to move toward faithfulness and can attempt to reconceive points of witness that seem to be at odds with Christian identity.

These factors combine to suggest a perspective and strategy by which today's church might draw upon some contemporary technologies.[10] The Christian community might identify some existential questions and issues that attract people's attention. The church can design programs and other acts of witness to address these concerns. Christian leadership can view such witnesses in a double way: as genuinely helpful events in their own rights, and as ports of entry through which to invite people into larger understandings of the world from a Christian perspective. The church can seek to help people with the specific issue, while helping them recognize the larger framework of the gospel within which to understand the issue.

Furthermore, Christian leaders need to recognize that people do not enter into Christian life full-grown. In a subtle but significant image, Christian theologians liken the water of baptism to the water of the womb; baptism is birth into the Christian family and the Christian worldview. The infant does not emerge from the mother's womb able to speak, read, and solve mathematical problems. The infant grows and matures gradually. In similar fashion, Christian consciousness grows developmentally, sometimes quite slowly and over a long period of time. Consequently, the church needs to fashion words and actions of witness that can meet people at their own stages of readiness to understand. And the church needs to create ways of helping people mature. It is unfair to suppose that a casual brush with the gospel will result in muscular Christian discipleship. We offer an example of this approach below by turning to the use of current interest in family life as a port of entry for persons of different generations into the gospel world.

The recognition of the contextuality of Christian witness brings both freedom and responsibility to the church and its leadership. Leaders are freed from the burden of feeling that every witness must be considered unfaithful if it does not measure up to the fullness of Christian vision. Even the best acts of witness almost inevitably contain concessions to creaturehood, sin, or other limitations. Recognizing that all witness inevitably has a corrupt edge, the church is freed to experiment with fresh forms of witness. Unsatisfactory forms of witness can be sent back to the drawing board, replaced, or scrapped without shame.

At the same time, the church is responsible always to be thinking critically about its witness. The church needs to "fit" its time and place. And it also needs to move in the direction of the criteria articulated below.

Criteria for Faithfulness

The simple fact that the church makes a witness (intentionally or unintentionally) does not automatically mean that it is a *Christian* witness. We now suggest three norms by which the church can begin to measure the adequacy of its Christian witness in any given occasion or form.[11]

1. *Appropriateness to the gospel.* The gospel is the center point of Christian identity. The life of the church, in all respects, is called to manifest God's unconditional love for all and God's will for justice for all. Witnesses that demonstrate such love and justice are consistent with the gospel and, therefore, appropriate to Christian identity. Witnesses that deny God's love or justice for any people or other created entities are inappropriate to the Christian community.

Leaders in the Christian community may find it helpful to ask a simple question of every aspect of the life of the church: Does this thought, proposal, or action demonstrate God's unconditional love for all and God's will for justice for all?

2. *Intelligibility.* The church must make a witness that is intelligible in the contemporary community. Intelligibility has three dimensions:

(1) The church's witness must be understandable. Those involved in the arena of the witness need to be able to get the point of the witness. For instance, a preacher may wax eloquent about justification by grace through faith. Each of these three terms is primary for Christian identity, but their nuances of meaning may be lost on today's biblically and theologically impaired congregations, and on those outside the congregation who may not be at all familiar with them. Hence, the preacher needs to explain justification, grace, faith, and their relationship.

(2) The church's testimony must be logically coherent. When the church's various statements and actions of witness contradict one another, the congregation does not know what to believe or how to act. Indeed, the credibility of the Christian witness is undercut. For instance, a church's witness is strengthened when it claims that it is a community of care and it actually shows care for visitors and others. The church's credibility is compromised when it claims to be a community of care but visitors and others do not experience care. Indeed, when visitors feel that they are means to an end, they may experience betrayal. A congregation may set a numerical goal for new members ("We want to receive 100 people into membership

this year") and consequently treat visitors as means to an end ("We need you to join our church so we can meet our goal").The result of such a witness is actually negative, as words and actions work against one another.

(3) The church's witness must make sense.That is, the Christian witness must be believable in the church's context.The church's claims about God and God's activity in the world cannot be unbelievable.[12]

This third point needs to be handled delicately.The worldviews of most communities in the West are ever changing in response to fresh perspectives and data. Furthermore, many Christian theologians today believe that the so-called Enlightenment (or modern) worldview that holds sway in many quarters is itself flawed and in need of reconstruction. Some aspects of current worldviews are actually opposed to the gospel. Hence, the compatibility of Christian witness with the contemporary perception of the world cannot become an imperial and unchallenged norm against which to measure the church's witness. At the same time, the church's witness must be credible to contemporary people in order for them to be willing to believe it and act upon it.

Today's international populace does not subscribe to a singular, universal perception of the world. In the contemporary era, we are ever more aware of a plurality of worldviews. Different communities operate out of different perspectives on the cosmos. In the last fifty years, philosophers and theologians have become increasingly aware of the fact that every community's point of view is an *interpretation* of the world.This recognition results in increasing awareness of relativity in all interpretations of life and the cosmos.This insight is the heart of the phenomena that are grouped under the heading "postmodernism."[13] Whereas "modern" citizens believed that they could locate the objective, undisputed facts of existence, many of today's citizens realize that all statements about reality are interpretive. Such statements represent a community's particular perception at a given moment in time and space.

The church finds itself in a climate of pluralism and relativism. Nonetheless, the church must offer a witness that is intelligible in the light of its best understanding of the world. At the same time, the church cannot woodenly regard its particular worldview as the imperial standard by which all other worldviews are to be measured.The church needs to remember that its perception of the cosmos is interpretive and, therefore, open to reformulation. This outlook gives the church a place to stand while it evaluates other ways of understanding the world. It also leaves the church with some elbow room to adjust its own worldview.

The authors of this book pose a simple criterion for this aspect of intelligibility. Christian witness ought to be able to be confirmed at some level of the community's experience. When the church asks people to disclaim what they otherwise think to be true, Christian witness moves into the realm of the nonintelligible and nonbelievable. At the same time, we recognize that experience is always interpreted. Hence, we need always to be open to fresh understanding of experience.

At the same time, we stress the possibility that Christian tradition may ask today's people to change their worldview. Christian affirmation may expose the inadequacy of current thinking; the church's witness may cause the community to enlarge or otherwise reshape its worldview.

The theological discipline of hermeneutics arose in order to help a present-day community find significance in past texts and traditions. Therefore, the church ought not dismiss aspects of its tradition too hastily in an attempt to make a witness in the mode of the present. Nonetheless, there are times when the church must transform its witness in order to make sense in the present.

3.   *Moral Plausibility*. The church must call for, and actualize, the moral treatment of all in its sphere of witness. The church must treat all things—animate and inanimate—as loved by God and as those for whom God seeks justice. For instance, in our time, many congregations make their buildings available for community service as acts of witness. These uses are all to the good when the groups that use a congregation's building exhibit God's love for all and God's will for justice for all. But the church becomes complicit in racism when it lends its building to a group that consciously or unconsciously sanctions racist attitudes and behaviors.

These three criteria yield three questions that the church can ask of every word or deed of Christian witness. Is this witness appropriate to the gospel? Is it intelligible? Is it morally plausible?

In some instances, the responses to these questions will be straightforward and their implications clear. "Yes. This act is an authentic witness to the gospel." "No. We cannot be implicated in such thinking or behavior." In other instances, the responses may not be as clear. Occasionally, the community may be left in ambiguity. In the latter case, the church identifies an interpretation that seems relatively satisfactory. Christians acknowledge the weak points of that interpretation. The church may discover that its witness is *relatively* faithful or relatively unfaithful. The church moves forward in witness with an eye ever toward ideas or circumstances or phenomena that may cause it to re-evaluate its witness.

The Distinctive Role of the Church

The question of the distinctive role of the church is initially quite easy to answer. The church is called to name the presence and purposes of the one Living God in the world, as it has come to know God through Jesus Christ. The church is not the only community in the world that understands itself to point to God. The church's kin—the synagogue and the mosque—witness to the same God. The distinctive role of the church is to testify to God as disclosed through Jesus Christ.

Naming God in the world is the one thing the church must do that it cannot count on any other body to do. Many other institutions help people and the cosmos by providing education, health care, therapy of various kinds, food, clothing, and other forms of life support. Many other communities provide rallying points for political action, systemic change in the larger social order, and even revolution. Many other groups address urgent issues ranging from the environmental crisis to cries for human liberation. Many are sympathetic to the church. Some other groups carry out activities that attempt to spread love and justice without recognition of the gospel or the church; a few such organizations are hostile to the church. But of all the human communities known to the writers of this book, only the church is specifically appointed to help the world community name God and the gospel in the world (as these are revealed through Jesus Christ) and to help the world community respond appropriately.

In these matters, the church needs a healthy humility. For the church does not have a monopoly on the divine presence. That is, the divine presence is found in places other than the church. God is omnipresent and always working for the good of everyone and everything in the cosmos. God is for all, even for those who do not know God, and even for those who deny God. God does not require a confession of faith and affiliation with the church in order for God to work for the good of a person or community. To be sure, God does not approve of all the attitudes and activities of people (and other creatures). God sometimes requires radical change (repentance). But God always aims for each created entity to achieve its highest potential. The vocation of the church is to testify to the universal presence and love of God, and to God's universal will for all to know justice. The church helps the world to recognize and name the Transcendent in the cosmos. The church cannot count on any other community to accomplish this task.

The church functions in the larger world much like the sacraments function in the church. The Lord's supper is an outward and visible sign of inward and spiritual grace. God uses the loaf and the cup as tangible vehicles to assure us of God's continuing goodwill toward us. When we receive them, we remember our responsibilities to live out our identities as beloved children of God who are called to testify to God's love for all and God's call for justice for all. Likewise, the church is an outward and visible sign of the presence and purposes of God. The life of the church is one way that God mediates the knowledge of the divine presence and purposes. The faithfulness of God to the church is a sign of God's faithfulness to all. The church's witnesses in word and deed should have a sacramental quality in helping the larger citizenry recognize and respond to divine love and enflesh the divine purpose of universal justice. The witness of the church is a way whereby the light of God shines in the world.

A caveat: The church alone cannot satisfy all the world's needs. The church rightly engages in acts of love and justice of the kind discussed here. The church wants to make as much impact as it can in personal and corporate life. But even the worldwide church is too small, and the problems of the cosmos too large, for the church to be able to solve all the world's problems by itself. Furthermore, other organizations are sometimes more efficient and more effective in addressing particular phenomena. The church needs to continue such ministries because of their sacramental character. The church's acts of care (e.g., feeding the hungry, demonstrating against racial injustice, providing shelters for abused women) are genuinely helpful. But the larger purpose of such actions is to embody God's concern for all. On the microscale, the church models how God wants all human communities to relate to problems on the macroscale. This recognition does not excuse the church from doing all that it can to provide help in specific situations. But it does relieve the church from excessive guilt and paralysis in the face of overwhelming need.

At the same time, the church does not have a monopoly on how to interpret the divine presence in the world. The church always offers the best interpretation of God's purposes that it can make within a given situation. But later reflection sometimes furnishes data that the church did not consider, or offers a fresh angle of vision, or exposes limitations in the church's perspective that the church did not previously recognize. From time to time the church discovers points at which the sacred traditions themselves need to be re-examined, reframed, or even reformulated. The church cannot *assume* that its pronouncements and points of view are inherently correct. Sometimes persons and communities from outside the church become agents who cause the church to discern aspects of the divine will that the church itself had misrepresented or missed.

To take an example, we know now that the Jewish and Christian traditions have long contained impulses toward women's liberation, but these remained largely suppressed or ignored until the contemporary era. The contemporary church became interested in women's liberation largely in response to urges for liberation that took popular form in secular culture. Such urges prompted the church to re-evaluate its own tradition and gospel with respect to women and to conclude that the gospel inclines toward liberation. Much the same thing is true about ecology. For centuries the church lent its interpretive authority to the industrialists who ravaged nature under the banner of exercising dominion. The church re-evaluated its teaching, in no small part, in response to the ecologists who called attention to the fact that human and natural survival were imperiled by the exploitation of nature. Hence, the church needs to reflect critically upon voices from outside its walls to listen for potential stirrings toward a refocused perception of God's love and justice.

The Church's Witness and Its Institutional Life

At the center of the church's interior life, the church is called to recognize and respond to God in ways that befit God's gracious love and clarion for justice. Leander Keck has recently pointed out that the church's life is grounded in acknowledging God's overflowing love and goodness. The awareness of the awesomeness of God draws forth "purposeless praise," that is, praise which has no purpose other than to honor God.[14] It has no ulterior motive. However, if the church is to be healthy enough to continue as a body and to make a witness beyond its parking lot, it needs to give attention to its institutional life.

Toward the end of helping the church do those things that are necessary to grow in spiritual maturity and strength for witness, Craig Dykstra has identified thirteen practices that ought to characterize the life of the congregation.

1. Worshiping God together—praising God, giving thanks for God's creative and redemptive work in the world, hearing God's word preached, and receiving the sacraments given to us in Christ.
2. Telling the Christian story to one another—reading and hearing the Scriptures and also the stories of the church's experience throughout history.
3. Interpreting together the Scriptures and the history of the church's experience, particularly in relation to their meaning for our own lives in the world.
4. Praying—together and by ourselves, not only in formal services but in all times and places.
5. Confessing our sin to one another, and forgiving and becoming reconciled with one another.

6. Tolerating one another's failures and encouraging one another in work each must do and the vocation each must live.

7. Carrying out specific faithful acts of service and witness together.

8. Suffering with and for each other and all whom Jesus showed to be our neighbors.

9. Providing hospitality and care, not only to one another but to strangers.

10. Listening and talking attentively to one another about our particular experiences in life.

11. Struggling together to become conscious of and understand the nature of the context in which we live.

12. Criticizing and resisting all those powers and patterns (both within the church and in the world as a whole) that destroy human beings, corrupt the human community, and injure God's creation.

13. Working together to maintain and create social structures and institutions which will sustain life in the world in ways that accord with God's will.[15]

With the exception of the last several practices, these qualities focus on what should happen inside the body of the church. Their nurture deserves the concentrated attention of minister and congregation. Unless they are functioning, the church will not be an optimal witnessing body.

However, a danger comes with these interior practices. Christians can easily let them become ends in themselves. The Christian community can become so self-absorbed in them that the community loses sight of the larger universe of purpose which congregational practice is to serve. For instance, a church's kitchen needs to be clean (for reasons of sanitation), but we have known congregations within which a select group functionally regards the kitchen as a Holy of Holies. Their mission becomes the preservation of the kitchen. They concentrate so much on maintaining the kitchen that they forget that a kitchen is designed to prepare food for hungry people. We know some clergy who appear to regard their vocations as "career tracks" on the same order as their counterparts in massive multinational corporations. We know some Christian leaders who seem to make a lifework out of massaging ecclesiastical machinery without conscious connection to the broader witness that machinery is intended to power.

When the church gives rightful attention to its internal practices, this life can itself be a witness. For the things that the church does and the way in which it does them can embody qualities of community life that can serve as a light for other communities in the world. The church can model personal and communal relationship, critical thinking, creative handling of disagreements, care for others (including the environment), steward- ship of money and physical resources. Persons and organizations in the general populace ought to be able to look at the church's life and think, "That is how we should live together."

The key point is that the attention the church gives to institutional life is not an end in itself but is for the purpose of witness.

These days, the long established churches are much absorbed with talk about renewal. This talk appears to be spurred by two factors. For one, many congregations in these denominations are lethargic and tired. Many congregations appear to be confused about what they are to do. Still others are fractious. The light is dim in many local communities of faith. Many congregations need to be renewed if they are to have vital witnesses.

The other factor is growing awareness of decline in traditional indi- cators of institutional success. Many congregations and denominations are getting smaller and older. Indeed, in our weekend travels to preach and teach in congregations, we find that many local communities of faith are composed primarily of retired or about-to-be-retired persons. Some of these churches are already on the margin of fiscal viability or are di- minishing in active membership to the point that it is difficult for them to carry on institutional life as they have for the past decades. Within a gen- eration or two, many of our ecclesial organizations will downsize greatly or will disappear. Some efforts at renewal appear to be aimed at institu- tional survival as such. One of us remembers a particularly poignant mo- ment at a clergy conference when a minister in the middle years of life all but wept in a plenary session, "I don't want to use the best years of my life and ministry to be a chaplain to a church in a hospice condition." The minister then made a plea for the church to create an evangelism strategy aimed at bringing a larger number of people into the church.

We approach this aspect of our discussion delicately. On the one hand, as we have noted, the church needs a healthy body in order to witness. A healthy body needs members who can perform the various functions needed by the body. The members themselves need to be in good health. The church needs to monitor its budget and its membership (who is joining, who is leaving) in order to be able to assess its capacity for wit- ness. On the other hand, the goal of the church is not just to keep its doors open. Indeed, when survival becomes a goal of the church, the witness of the church can be subverted. Christians can regard persons outside the church as means to the church's end of survival. Persons become resources to help pay the church's bills, to staff the church's committees, to fill the pews to give the impression that the congregation is a success. When people become means to the church's ends, the credibility of the gospel and the church are undermined.

We hope that people will be attracted to church when the church is engaged in dynamic mutual critical correlation of the gospel to the situation of its context. Institutional success may result from faithful witness. But there are no guarantees that statistical success will follow such correlation. And in some cases, authentic witness can actually discourage people from wanting to identify with the church. However, institutional success, as measured by traditional indicators of membership and program and financial contributions, may result from peddling cheap grace, or offering a watered-down gospel as the formula to happiness, or skillful technological manipulation void of any real theological message. This matter is also delicate because human motives are seldom pure. Even the strongest desire to witness faithfully to the gospel can be compromised by slight but still self-serving, even self-righteous, inclinations. In any event, the church needs to interpret its life through a powerful lens of humility.

The Church's Ministry in the Next Twenty Years

This book is prompted, in part, by the fact that the church is in a time of transition. Many assumptions and formulae for church life that have carried the church through the better part of the twentieth century are no longer working as successfully as they did. Christian leaders can view this time of transition in one of two ways. The church can weep, wail, gnash our teeth, and feel homesick for the 1950s (or some other time that we recall as the golden era of ecclesiastical life). Or the church can view this transitional period as an exciting, if risky, adventure that calls forth our best energies.

We opt for the latter. When we began our ministries (Clark was ordained in 1961, Ron in 1974), we assumed that the church would probably continue in its then-current institutional form for the foreseeable future. The ministry was exciting, or we would not have gone into it. And the church certainly offered opportunities for innovation and change. But to be honest, at a deep level we thought that a minister was largely a caretaker whose job was to manage a congregation whose existence was secure. The church could almost take it for granted that its place in North American culture would bring a steady, if not always lavish, flow of new members onto the rolls.

As is well known, these assumptions are no longer true. In the pluralistic and relativistic culture of late twentieth-century North America, the church exists alongside other institutions in the marketplace of human loyalties. The church must win interest and commitment afresh in each generation, or its witness will continue to diminish.

In the transitional situation of the church today, what ministers do (or do not do) has a direct effect on whether the church has the possibility to be re-energized, or whether we go on with business as usual, and diminishing returns. A lot is at stake.

This situation calls for our best efforts. But the current generation does not have a handy manual of ideas and programs that are all but guaranteed to develop a vital witnessing community in the next twenty years. We must discover fresh forms of ecclesial life and witness for the many situations in which the church finds itself today. This process can be electric with excitement. Doubtless it will have moments fraught with angst and uncertainty. Along the way, the church will probably have to pause at the cemetery of failure to bury some attempts that die. But the prevailing ethos can be one of adventure. For like the heroes of *Star Trek*, today's church is going where no church in recent memory has gone. The church needs to be able to discover and develop modes of life and witness that are appropriate to the gospel, intelligible, morally plausible, and suited to the world at the turn of the millennia.

What is necessary for the church to make its way forward? We identify six necessary qualities and approaches. *First,* the church must have a normative theological vision that has a clear understanding of the nature and purpose of the church. We identified such a vision earlier in this chapter. Without such a polar star, the church can get lost among any number of the lesser gods, gospels, and luminaries that are passing through the world today. The church needs to be constantly reminding itself of this vision (and the church needs always to be reflecting on the adequacy and fittingness of its vision).

Second, the church needs to understand the situations in which the church finds itself. In particular, it needs to have a grasp of what is happening, and why (insofar as possible), and what is needed in the light of its normative theological vision.

We introduce an example that we will follow through the remainder of these steps. Many families in the United States today are under great stress. Few families fulfill Luther's hope that the household can be an arena in which all grow in the gospel. Indeed, the dynamics in some homes today mediate a deformed image of love. They sanction injustice, and even mutual abuse of the household members. People need help to know how to relate to one another in love and justice. Unhealthy family situations result in part from the individual behaviors and attitudes of family members, but they are also deeply affected by larger factors at work in our social system that put stress on family life. In order for family units to function optimally, changes need to occur in the larger social forces in our culture. Hence, the church that tries to help people relate better within their homes performs a service, but only a partial one. The church needs to witness for more loving and just patterns in our larger social fabric.

Third, the church needs to envision strategies of ministry that have a good chance of helping the church develop a vital life and witness. At the present cultural juncture, the church particularly needs imagination. The Christian community needs to conceive fresh ways to offer the gospel to people outside the congregation. The church also needs to imagine fresh ways of corporate Christian life that are less attuned to the institutional management approach to church life characteristic of the middle years of this century and more oriented toward providing the opportunities for growth, service, and relationship that are characteristic of this transitional period.

As we suggested earlier, the church can often make use of points of felt need in order to try to attract people's interest. For example, many Boomers and Gen 13ers are now parents who are vitally interested in family life. A congregation can often appeal to this interest by offering programs that help families develop healthy relationships. This appeal becomes a port through which the church can invite parents and families into the gospel world.

On such an occasion the church must provide hands-on perspectives and skills for day-to-day household attitudes and behaviors. The church would want to offer people the opportunity to discover connections between the love and justice needed in the family and the love and justice of the gospel. In addition, the church would hope that people could be introduced to the systemic factors at work in our society, and the church's efforts to witness to changes necessary to move toward a world of love and justice.

Concurrently, the church needs to realize that youthful mom and dad may not be ready to launch a campaign to reshape North American culture as a result of a single Saturday morning forum on family life. These people may not have been in church for years. But their parental aspirations cause them to respond to a congregation's ad in a neighborhood newspaper or to a flier mailed to their home. When they walk in the door the first time, they may not be ready to grasp the relationship between macro social forces and their micro day-to-day (but immensely important) household relationships. They need opportunities to grow.

Fourth, the church needs to mobilize the skills necessary to translate its dreams into actual acts of ministry. The pastor will undoubtedly be a key figure in this process. However, the minister will not likely have (or be able to acquire) all the skills that are necessary for mobilizing a congregation for new forms of ministry. In any event, the leadership of this task will call for more time and energy than a single pastor can have. Nor is the pastor always the best person to be the chief administrator of these efforts.

This process will likely be one in which the notion of the church as the *body* of Christ comes into play. Lay leadership will need to provide key elements of vision and energy. And the fact of the matter is that most congregations contain lay leaders who are more skilled than their clergy at administration and at working with other people. Furthermore, lay-people are often more responsive to other laypeople, when it comes to making changes in congregational life, than they are to the pastor. Granted, the pastor needs to be involved in the process. But we think pastors will ordinarily make their optimum contributions less as key players who perform the "hands-on" activities of witness, and more as coaches. When a process of change is underway, the key contribution of the minister is to lead the community in reflecting theologically on the process of change that is unfolding. The particular gift that ministers bring to the body is theological consciousness.

Some ministers are extroverts who have a natural inclination to want to work with people on organizational matters from day to day. However, many clergy tend to be more introverted than extroverted; they tend to be more oriented to thinking and reflecting on issues of meaning than toward mobilizing for action. Hence, when they are on the front line of dealing with people in administrative roles, day after day, they act out of character. Even those introverted clergy who learn how to lead effectively often find such processes emotionally grueling.

This role will require a major change of self-perception on the part of many clergy. Many clergy in the long-established denominations today are more oriented to doing things themselves than to raising up leadership from within the congregation to take responsibility for processes of change or for particular ministries. Clergy end up making endless phone calls, perpetually recruiting, even setting up the tables and chairs for meetings. Along the way, their particular gifts are lost. Not surprisingly, many ministers burn out. Clergy need to take seriously the admonition of Ephesians "to equip the saints for the work of ministry, for building up the body of Christ" (Ephesians 4:12).

In some cases, a congregation will not contain persons in its membership or immediate circle of supporters who have the skills necessary for a particular ministry. Hence, the church may need self-consciously to enlarge its circle of friends and to seek help from persons or organizations beyond its current range of acquaintances. It may also need to buy help in order to be able to tap the skills necessary for a particular act of ministry.

Returning to the example of the church that seeks to reach people through appeal to concern for family life—the church needs to find leaders who can help families develop the perspectives and skills that are important to healthy family life. And the church needs to employ creative ways to invite those who are most likely to respond positively to such an offering. The church needs to use a sensitive spirit in assessing the degree to which persons who respond to such events are ready to explore family life in the light of formative theological realities such as sin, grace, and the larger purposes of God. But the church needs to find ways to help participants name connections between the gospel and their familial situations. The church needs also to offer follow-up possibilities in order to facilitate continued growth.

(5)   *Fifth,* the church needs to evaluate the degree to which actual acts of ministry are consistent with the normative theological vision and are received positively within the church and by the inhabitants of the larger social context in which the church makes its witness. The church asks itself: Which aspects of this witness seem to work? Why do they work? Which aspects of this witness seem not to work? Why do they not work? What do we learn from this evaluation that we think we want to continue? What do we learn from this evaluation that we think we want to try differently?

In connection with a family life workshop, the church should provide a mechanism (perhaps in the form of an evaluation form filled out by participants) for immediate feedback. Some weeks or months later, the church may also want to follow through with a home visit or other form of feedback to ask participants to assess the effect of the event and to offer suggestions for improving similar events in the future. Further, the church can try to observe the effects of the family life event on families. Are improved forms of relationship coming to visible expression? (Such data are quite "soft" and may not be expressed outside the privacy of the home, but visibly improved relationships in public places may result and would be an encouragement to the planners of the event). The church leadership can also assess who came, who did not. Is it possible to determine why? And what do we learn for advertising, focus, the conduct of the event itself that we want to repeat? To change?

(6)   *Sixth,* the church needs to integrate what it has learned from its process of evaluation into its ongoing life. When analysis of its ministries indicates the need for modifying (even completely retooling or eliminating) particular witnesses, the community of faith needs to change some of

its practices in order to try to minimize obstacles to ministry and to maximize opportunities for witness.

The church needs to recognize that the above process needs to be continually ongoing. In the foreseeable future, the church community will be in constant flux (at least in some aspects of its life) in analysis, experimentation, evaluation, modification, and subsequent re-experimentation, re-evaluation, re-modification. The church will seldom get an act of witness completely "right." And even when the church gets it "right" in connection with a particular act of ministry, that "rightness" cannot likely be repeated in exactly the same way again and again and again.

How Change Occurs

As most local pastors know, long-established congregations are sometimes reluctant to change familiar patterns of thinking and behaving. Once in a while a dramatic event or insight will cause a congregation to make a large-scale change in a very short time in some aspect of its witness. However, change usually takes place in small, incremental steps over a fairly long period of time. What are the conditions necessary for change to occur in the typical congregation?

The foundational quality necessary in a congregation's life for change to take place (whether in lightning-like moments or over time) is trust in God. When a community is secure in its awareness of the divine presence, it can be secure enough to take the risks that often accompany innovations in ecclesial life. A mature church will know that the recognition of God's presence does not guarantee success or ward off conflict or failure. But the affirmation of God-with-us reminds the church that it is not alone in the world; the church is always in the company of the Transcendent Other. Furthermore, in the most difficult moments of life in the church, the cognizance of the divine presence gives us perspective within which to acknowledge the relativity of our successes and failures.

A correlate, of course, is that the members of the church need to trust one another. Adult learners are most available to their teachers and to the subject matter that they study when they trust the teacher. A church is much the same way. The members of a congregation are more available to entertain new and different ideas when they trust one another and when they trust the minister than when they feel unrecognized by others or distrustful of others. Hence, one of the most important pastoral approaches to encourage a climate that has a likelihood of being ready for change is to develop relationships of trust in the community and between the community and God.

People are often receptive to change when they recognize some need for change. In the language of our colleague D. Bruce Roberts, people are willing to think about change when they perceive that their world is no longer in equilibrium. On the negative end of the spectrum, members are sometimes ready to entertain notions of change when they see that something is not working and say, "We need to do something." A congregation that is on the edge of reading its own obituary is sometimes willing to try new approaches to congregational life to prolong its life. On the positive end of the spectrum, a strong and vital community is often pulled forward into change when it catches sight of a vision that offers the possibility that good things can become even better. A congregation that built a new building just a decade ago may build again in order to accommodate crowds that are increasing in geometric proportion. Whether by force of need or lure of vision, or some point in between, the congregation needs to become aware of the desirability of new forms of ministry.

Some congregations are able to recognize the need for change in modes of witness and to implement changes throughout the congregational system. Other congregations find that while the community as a whole realizes the importance of adapting to new situations, some in the congregation are unwilling to amend their present styles of life and witness. These people are willing to have new opportunities for others, but they would like to continue in their familiar ways. Such congregations are often able to work out a program of congregational life that maintains (with quality) the existing life while inaugurating new expressions of life and witness. In such cases, it is important for the various members of the body to remember their connectedness with one another. In a few instances, certain people or groups within congregations will not budge. At that point, the community needs to decide whether the whole of its life will be governed by the decisions and behavior of a few. If the congregation as a whole decides to make changes that cause a few to lament, and even leave, the community needs to take every opportunity to demonstrate its continuing love and respect.

Leaders in situations of long-term change often need large infusions of patience. Pastors and other visionaries are often ready for new worlds to burst fully developed from the womb of imagination. But incremental gains often come in very small contractions. Leaders in the community of faith need to be willing to take a long-term view on what needs to happen. We have found it helpful to give thanks for every willingness to change, no matter how small, no matter how seemingly insignificant in the light of the movement needed. Every gain is a gain. Over the course of long and faithful ministries, such gains add up. In the course of change, nearly every leader is visited by frustration, disappointment, and pain. At such times, endurance is paramount.

Patience needs to be accompanied by persistence. The inertia present in some congregational systems is of epic proportions. Pastors and future-oriented leaders need to monitor the balance between moving at a speed that enables most in the congregation to change comfortably and the persistence needed to keep the congregation moving. Forward thinkers need to have a sense of when to press the accelerator and when to let up. But they need to find ways to keep issues for change alive in the congregation's consciousness.

At times, of course, ministers and others need to be bold. Incremental change is not always sufficient. In a context where a congregation perceives a yearning need, or is attracted to a possibility of great promise, a bold vision can often capture the commitment of the community. In other contexts, in which perception of the need or possibility for change is low, a bold vision itself can awaken the imaginations of the community as to what is possible and desirable.

Change in congregational life cannot be produced by the application of a simple formula. In planning for change, pastoral wisdom is often decisive. A faithful and insightful minister often has a sense of where the congregational traffic is flowing on these issues. Clergy often know how much change the bridges of congregational life can bear. They can often perceive the strategies of change that will best work as a community attempts to travel into the new century.

Conclusion

This chapter emphasizes the pervasive need for theological analysis of all aspects of the church's consideration of new technologies and other dimensions of ecclesial life. In the subsequent chapters, we move from the general theological question of "What is the nature and purpose of the church?" to specific implications of our response to that question in four modes of witness: worship, teaching, *koinonia*, and service. We consider each mode of ministry in light of the purpose of the church and the criteria for discerning an appropriate Christian way of life. We turn next to the central event of the church's life—worship—and to preaching, one of the pivotal moments of worship. We then consider the educational ministry of the church, approaches to service, and the fellowship dimension of the church's life.

3

An Intense Teaching and Learning Community

Loren B. Mead, in his book *More Than Numbers,* deals with the congregational decline caused by the fact that members simply "drop out" of the congregation. The effort to reclaim those who have dropped out is largely fruitless, he argues, and the energy involved in doing so would be better spent elsewhere. Specifically, it is better to work on preventing dropouts than to pursue those who have left.[1] Sociological studies show that many of those who have dropped out were not particularly piqued or disenchanted; "they simply find life outside the church attractive and relatively fulfilling. For them, the *need* for church is not convincing, nor are there as many forces in society encouraging or supporting church membership."[2]

What churches should do, he suggests, is to "build strong, challenging communities of faith, communities that will stretch and empower congregational members." Where this kind of congregation exists, participation in church life will itself be fascinating and satisfying.[3] An important key to creating this kind of energizing community of faith is providing an environment for what Mead calls the "maturational growth" of members of the congregation. Maturational growth is "growth in faith and in the ability to nurture and be nurtured."[4]

49

Teaching and Learning as Signs of a Vital Congregation

What makes for such growth is the topic of this chapter. Growth in faith, we suggest, has several components to it that need to be intentionally nurtured in the congregation. Because there is no faith that is not in some way understood or interpreted, since to interpret *is* to understand, growth in faith means growth in understanding one's faith. It also means growth in discipleship, in living out one's faith in society. One of the oldest definitions of theology, handed down by Augustine and Anselm, among others, is that theology is "faith seeking understanding." Every Christian, at whatever stage of his or her development in the Christian faith, has some understanding of that faith. In this sense, every Christian has a theology. Every Christian also, however frequently or infrequently, also comes upon occasions when she thinks about her faith and, in this sense, "does theology." However well or poorly we understand faith, we all have some understanding of it; and however well or poorly we do theology, we all do it. In every case, the very human quest to understand what one believes, indeed even to know what one believes, can and should be fostered by the church.

Why should a pastor of a congregation take it as a priority to create a learning congregation, one that is intensely involved in deepening and sharpening its understanding of the Christian faith? Let us here pose some answers to this question. First, the Christian faith itself is not some amorphous "feeling" that we all have but cannot express or can express, but in highly individualized and variegated ways. To be a Christian is to be able to think, talk, and act in Christian ways. Christian faith has to be learned; it is a learned behavior—a way of talking and a way of acting. To be sure, it involves feeling or affect, as well. Nonetheless, how we feel is shaped by the language we use. We express our feelings in language, to be sure, but those feelings are already shaped by the language we use. Feelings and taste can and must be educated.

One reason, indeed the primary reason, that we have congregations and that congregations have teachers (whether ordained or not) is that Christian faith has to be learned. If Christian faith has to be learned, who else is to teach it other than the Christian community? We claimed in the first chapter that the time is long past when the church can rely on other institutions in the society to do this job. Only the church can be counted on to do the job that only the church is given and called to do, and that is to make Christians out of people. Christian families may do it, of course, but it is quite rare that we find such families living on deserted islands and not participating in some church.

What we mean by making Christians out of people is that the church has the responsibility to help its members come to understand themselves as Christians and to develop the habits or practices necessary to be Christians and to act in Christian ways in relation to their neighbors. The church is called to help us understand the world we live in, in its ultimate dimensions, and to help us live in the world that we so understand. It is given and called to help us understand who we are as Christians and what that means for how we intend and act toward our neighbors and toward the larger world of humanity and nature. To do this is not only to come into possession of a certain set of values, but also to develop the character that results from the habitual practice of talking and acting in Christian ways. The mission of the church in the world is to spread the love of God and the love of neighbor and to do this in both word and deed. But it is well to remember that this is, finally, done by Christian people whom the church must equip for the task of living by grace and living out an ethic of grace.

Further reasons why the church should take upon itself the urgent task of teaching the Christian faith are easily adduced. In their book *The Congregation: Sign of Hope*, Chris Hobgood and Ann Updegraff-Spleth spell out what they call "five systems that will be active elements in a congregation that knows and cares about its mission."[5] Every vital congregation will have "a unified self-image" and not be simply a collection of "fragmented parts." Here the authors envision a congregation on the Pauline metaphor of the "body of Christ" in which "interdependence and shared growth" characterize the whole, and each person's role is valued and cherished. But how do we arrive at some such unified self-image? How is a congregation composed, at least to some extent, of people who tacitly view themselves as the consumers or customers of religion transformed into a community committed to being the embodiment of Christ in the world? They have to come to learn to see themselves that way, to talk of themselves that way, and to begin to act that way. In the all-too-typical case, the pastor and a few others may talk of the church's being the "body of Christ," but this kind of talk quickly evaporates when board and committee meetings occur.

Hobgood and Updegraff-Spleth secondly stipulate that a vital congregation will manifest "shared ownership of congregational life and mission."[6] This is a way of making more explicit what was involved in a congregation's having a unified self-image. A congregation needs to plan its life (and its budget!) in terms of a shared sense of mission. They suggest that the way it gets to such a consensus is by cataloging the tacit understandings of mission held by different members, spotting the "points of

convergence" among them, framing a mission statement that sets a course for the congregation and planning its life together in the light of that statement. That is all well and good, but it will work much better if the congregation is engaged in theological study and reflection on the mission of the church in general and in some consideration and analysis of its own opportunities for mission. That the congregation should be actively involved in mission may itself come as a surprise to those who regard themselves as the primary beneficiaries of the congregation's efforts at ministry.

Further, Hobgood and Updegraff-Spleth suggest that the best model for leadership in a congregation is one that they call "flexible." By this they mean that such leadership is "open," ready to enhance the ministry of others, "strategic" (having a vision), and "shared" (evoking the gifts of others).[7] By definition, leadership in most congregations (other than those that are still run by an authoritarian system) needs to be flexible. This is true, if for no other reason, because most congregations heavily involve and rely on lay leadership drawn from all groups and ages in the church. Even traditionally episcopal systems of church governance increasingly entail and depend upon significant involvement of lay leadership. Congregational systems of self-government presuppose an educated laity, a laity that is shaped by the biblical vision and capable of theological conversation about what it is given and called to do. Where this assumption does not hold, the most open and flexible leadership will constantly be frustrated, particularly if it is also motivated by some authentic vision of what the church is given to be and to become. Hence, flexible leadership cannot afford to be flexible on the issue of whether or not its deliberating bodies have learned the language and practices of the Christian faith. Besides, what pastor, who can be dismissed by the governing board, would like to have a board that does not understand the Christian faith and the purpose of the church?

Next, a robust congregation will manifest "spiritual vitality."[8] Here the authors make a comment to which we must demur. They say that spiritual vitality "really has nothing to do with the type of theology a congregation shares or the way it prays and worships." It is not difficult to think of types of theology or ways of praying and worshiping that would most decidedly sap the spiritual vitality of persons and congregations. Just to say that theology is unimportant (as some church-growth or vital-church experts do) implies that there are no more and no less authentic and, hence, invigorating or rejuvenating ways of understanding it. Would a woman's spiritual vitality be sapped if she were steadily exposed to a sexist theology? Would minority groups feel welcome in a congregation whose theology was compatible with racism? Would someone deeply committed to Jesus Christ as the "Prince of Peace" be gladdened by uncritical support for each and every war that comes along? Would the person weighed down by loneliness or anxiety find spiritual comfort in a congregation that did not make it plain and concretely evident that God's grace is sufficient to all our needs? There are ways of misunderstanding and, hence, missing the Christian faith. As an example of this, some midwest churches in the early 1920s found it theologically permissible to welcome the Klan into their fellowship. They were not, however, spiritually vital.

What Hobgood and Updegraff-Spleth probably had in mind with their statement was that it is neither possible nor desirable to seek some enforced and homogenized theological agreement on the finer points of doctrine in the congregation. That is not only so, but necessary if there is to be freedom to think and mature spiritually. But there must be at least enough of a common vision to nurture a theological conversation within the congregation.

The last factor identified is what Hobgood and Updegraff-Spleth call "mission over maintenance." Mission is acceptance of the call to serve others; maintenance is "doing the work to stay alive." In such difficult times as the present, it is tempting and easy for a congregation to get trapped in the maintenance syndrome; for it, mission will always take a back seat to paving the parking lot and repairing the roof. In some congregations, it seems that getting around to serving the purpose of the church will have to be infinitely delayed because the building will never get any younger. Nor will a congregation committed to such a tedious agenda ever itself get any younger, since it is difficult to attract people to do nothing more than pick up their share of someone else's electricity bill.

A maintenance-oriented congregation needs to be reoriented around the gospel of Jesus Christ. This will not happen by wishing for it or waiting on some magical event to make it take place. Let us put it this way: babies do not come into the world preprogrammed to live out an insipid agenda of building-maintenance. A congregation, in its style of life, *teaches* people that this is what they should be most concerned with if they are to be "responsible" Christians. In how many congregations is the message implicitly communicated that the "really responsible" people, the ones with their eye on the prize, are always talking about the need for new carpeting and repaving the parking lot? Alternatively put, maintenance-orientation is a *learned* style of Christian life. It can be *unlearned*; not easily perhaps, but it can. Similarly, the lesson conducive to great spiritual vitality that can be *learned* (and hence must be taught) is that *money follows mission.* When a congregation is genuinely excited about its mission and when the building is increasingly seen as a necessary tool to getting the mission accomplished, there will always be enough money to replace the heating unit in the kindergarten classroom. This is particularly so if it understands education as central to its mission. But a congregation knowing this and understanding it deep down is a theologically mature congregation that did not get that way by accident.

Resembling the Synagogue

At the end of the first war with Rome (years 68–73 of the first century C.E.), the temple in Jerusalem was destroyed and the religion of biblical Israel with its priests and sacrificial cult passed from the scene of history. Judaism in the form in which we know it today—with a synagogue, rabbis and dedication to the study of the Torah—arose from the ashes of biblical religion. Few Christians are aware that, just like Christianity, so too Judaism was born in the first century. The elements out of which it recreated itself were already in place, but they were lifted up into prominence and set in a new configuration in the reshaping of the community of faith.

This new religion had as its institution not a temple but a synagogue (the word literally means "gathering" or "congregation," but like "church" has come to be associated with a building). The synagogue is a "house of study" (*beth midrash*). The new kind of religious leader was not a priest but a rabbi (a term meaning "teacher"). A rabbi was and is an ordinary member of the people of God who has both the talent and education necessary to be a teacher of the faith. And Judaism had as its focus not a temple cult, but study of the Torah, worship, and deeds of loving-kindness. When it works as it is supposed to, the rabbi is the chief (but not the only) teacher in an intense teaching/learning community of faith.

Because the synagogue has never in its two-thousand-year history been culturally or politically "established," as the church was throughout the history of Christendom (roughly from 325 to 1800 legally, and even longer popularly), it never could or did assume that society at large would do its job for it. Jews had to tell the story God gives and calls them to live by if they were going to be able to live by the story that they told. There is a reason that Jewish children learn Hebrew in after-school classes, study Jewish history and civilization, dress up and have fun with noisemakers at Purim when the story of Esther is read, and can conduct the synagogue service in Hebrew and make a statement on the meaning of Jewish faith at their *bar mitzvah* or *bat mitzvah* ceremonies. Christians who want to see outstanding examples of congregational education in action should visit some *bar mitvah* and *bat mitzvah* services (*bar mitzvah* services are for boys, typically about the age of thirteen; *bat mitzvah* services are for girls).

One thing that Judaism has always appreciated is its own identity as a people called by God to walk on the Way of Life and thereby be a witness to the Gentiles. Of the covenant that God graciously made with the people Israel through Moses on Sinai, scripture tells us that God said: "today... I have set before you...life and death, blessings and curses. Choose life so that you and your descendants may live..." (Deuteronomy 30:19). Abraham was the first character in the Bible to be "called" by God, much as Jesus later called some Galileans to be his disciples and follow him on the Way of Life. God promised to Abraham: "In you all the families of the earth [i.e., all the Gentiles] shall be blessed" (Genesis 12:3). Christians confess that Jesus Christ is God's "Yes!", God's "Amen!" to this promise: "For in him every one of God's promises is a 'yes'" (2 Corinthians 1:20). So it was when Mary and Joseph presented Jesus in the temple at Jerusalem, Simeon sang to God: "for my eyes have seen your salvation, which you have prepared in the presence of all peoples, a light for revelation to the Gentiles and for glory to your people Israel" (Luke 2:30–32).

Called to walk in the way (*torah* means "way" and "teaching") and to witness to God for the benefit of the world, Jews have always known and appreciated their distinctness from society and culture at large. Stanley Hauerwas and William Willimon report on a rabbi in Greenville, South Carolina, who commented: "It's tough to be a Jew in Greenville. We are forever telling our children, 'That's fine for everybody else, but it's not fine for you. You are special. You are different. You are a Jew. You have a different story. A different set of values."[9] Churches, pastors, and Christian parents need to learn to say the same thing to their young people, say Hauerwas and Willimon: "Such behavior is fine for everyone else, but not fine for you. You are special. You are different. You have a different story. You have a different set of values. You are a Christian."[10]

The upshot of this, for the task and joy of becoming a teaching/ learning congregation, is that it makes an incredible difference in how we go about the task of being the church. Being a Christian or, better, *becoming* a Christian, is not something that happens accidentally, haphazardly, or naturally. It does not happen to people just because they grow up in North America; it may have once, to a great extent, but no longer. Christians are purposefully created, shaped, formed by a church that realizes that if it does not create Christians, nobody will. The church needs to be more like the synagogue—"a faith community that does not ask the world to do what it can only do for itself."[11]

Resembling the Rabbi

The reason why, in Protestantism, we have ordained ministers is to see to it that the preaching and teaching of the word of God are not left up to chance. Because we have a mediator with God in Jesus Christ, said the great reformers Luther and Calvin, we do not need another mediator in the person of a priest. Because we affirm the priesthood of all believers, we can all mediate the love of God to one another and receive the love of God from one another and from the neighbor. Why then do we need ordained ministers?

The best answer to this question from the Reformers was provided by John Calvin: "Nothing fosters mutual love more fittingly than for men [he could have said: 'and women'] to be bound together with this bond: one is appointed pastor to teach the rest."[12] It is through teaching of the Christian faith that the "renewal of the saints is accomplished . . . [and] the body of Christ is built up." The Reformation understanding of the priesthood of all believers, along with the Reformed insistence on self-governing congregations, presupposes a laity that is well educated in the Christian faith. In Calvin's view, the functions of the apostles, prophets, and evangelists of the early church were temporary. We no longer have apostles and prophets (there are people who speak prophetically today, to be sure, but in the New Testament church prophets spoke words of the risen Christ to the community).

Every pastor is given and called to be a teacher of the Christian faith to the community of faith. This does not mean that the pastor is the *only* teacher of the Christian faith in the community. It does mean that with regard to teaching the buck stops at the pastor's desk. Many of us grew up in churches in which we learned a lot about the Christian faith from Mrs. Martin and Mr. Mayo, from the young Reverend Smith who organized the youth group for two years and took us on work projects and to summer camp, from the layman who befriended the kids in the church and took them bowling on Sunday afternoon, from the congregational elders who taught us how to pray from the heart, and from the wide variety of people from whom we learned how they coped with the vicissitudes of life and death by being able to see them through the eyes of faith. In a well-functioning church everybody is a teacher of the Christian faith.

But for pastors it is critically important to reclaim this role. It is back there in the tradition, not so far removed in time in mainline congregations, just a few generations back. It is over there in the synagogue, where the rabbi does it quite well. A few books ago, we suggested that if congregations were to become vital centers of the *practice* of Christian faith, pastors needed to reconsider the possibilities in the role model of the *rabbi*, chief teacher and spiritual leader of the congregation.[13] The job of pastor is, by its nature, a rabbinical function. It is no accident that in the gospels Jesus is addressed some forty-two times as rabbi or "teacher." We could learn something from this fact.

Since the 1950s pastoral "identity" has gone through several stages. For many the 1960s were a period of crisis: people were leaving the ministry, the "death of God" theology was afoot, and pastors wondered just exactly what they were supposed to do. In the 1970s many pastors began to see themselves as "professionals," as if in adopting a model from the legal and medical fields they could find one apt for themselves. Some devoted themselves to careers in pastoral psychotherapy (a fine field in itself, but not a good paradigm for a congregational minister) and thought that this would give them some status that they were otherwise denied. But they were looking for status in all the wrong places. There was plenty of it available in being a teacher of the Christian faith, and a clear role-definition as well.

Lately some pastors, still unclear about what they are given and called to do, want to be "facilitators," a term that is utterly elusive in meaning when one seeks to pin it down and find out what its user intends by it. It seems to be a way of saying to a congregation, "I don't know what we ought to be doing here, but if any of you has an idea I'll facilitate it." Or, as a friend in the pastorate puts it, "I don't know that tune, but if you'll whistle a few bars I'll learn to dance to it." Other folk go into the ministry because they "need to be needed" and spend their ministerial careers *reactively* responding to whatever needs come across the telephone or over the transom. After a couple of decades of this, they wonder why they are "burned out" in ministry. The answer is obvious: without a vision, a sense of direction, and a clear identity of one's pastoral vocation, a facilitative, reactive pastor gets jerked every which way from Sunday to Sunday and never has a sense of accomplishment or success.

Possibly the first step toward revitalizing a congregation is for the pastor to become deeply intentional about taking up the task of being a teacher of the Christian faith in and with that community. The pastor can model for the congregation what it means to be a mature Christian, to think about matters of import from a Christian point of view, to catalyze others and empower them to talk the language of Christian faith, to give congregants an alternative way of speaking about persons and issues than they are exposed to on talk radio or television talk shows. In a vibrant, teaching/learning congregation that gets serious about its mission of nurturing people in the faith and transforming the world from injustice toward justice, the pastor is the central, but not the only, teacher. And in such a context, other kinds of pastoral responsibilities, such as seeing to institutional maintenance and providing crisis intervention therapy, have some point and purpose to them and are works of grace and love.

Making Actual the Priesthood of All Believers

We talk much, in Protestantism and other communities of faith, of the "priesthood of all believers." At one time this was an expression full of content and meaning, a way of naming all the members of a congregation and saying of them that they all could and should have a vital ministry because of their baptism. Ministry is shared in an egalitarian way among all members of the community, and the role of the ordained clergy was to "equip the saints." Equipping the saints meant so seeing to it that Christians were educated in the Christian faith that they could, in fact, engage in Christian conversation with one another, pray for one another, do deeds of loving-kindness toward one another and their neighbors, be active teachers of the Christian faith, and carry out the ministry of the church in the world.

But in a congregation that has long ignored the teaching task, where hardly anybody has darkened the door of a Sunday school classroom since they were in high school, and where the capacity to speak the language of the Christian faith and engage in its nurturing and transformative practices, the phrase "the priesthood of all believers" has been emptied of all significance. When this happens, the "priesthood of all believers" has only the silly meaning that all members of the congregation are equal in authority when speaking on any matter, regardless of whether they are educated in the Christian faith. In a congregation that does not engage in the theological education of its members, this means that the lay voice tends to reflect the opinions of the culture at large.

This can lead to considerable stress and conflict in the congregation, as happens in a board meeting when every variety of view is heard on an issue except for any that is recognizably Christian. Further, in such a situation, there are few resources for putting the situation right and beginning to look at difficult and emotional issues from the point of view of the mission to which Christ calls the church. The "bottom line" takes precedence over the purpose.

The church can no longer so take itself for granted. Never should it have done so, but the insight available to us now is that, in any case, we no longer can. If we are to make actual what the phrase "the priesthood of believers" points to, the congregation must become an intense teaching/learning community. Further, if revitalization of the mainline churches is to occur, it will not happen from the top down, from the national and judicatory leadership, but from the bottom up, from congregations. It will happen there or not at all. National and judicatory leadership can help, and we know some who are working hard and faithfully at it but they cannot take the place of the local congregation.

When the public (that is, within the congregation) ministry of preaching and teaching the Christian faith, of passing on and creatively and appropriately revising the Christian legacy of faith, does not happen in the church, "the church slips back into the world to become nothing more than the world."[14] The kind of language spoken in the board meeting is a good barometer of the extent to which this has happened in a congregation.

The antidote to this situation and the way to make actual the priesthood of all believers is to have an intense program of the theological education of laypeople in the congregation. We have defined theology simply as "faith seeking understanding." That is, theology is part of the understanding life of every believer. For some strange and inexplicable reason, theology has been restricted to those who wish to become clergy. Somehow it is important that the Reverend Smith understand the Christian faith, but not important for Mr. Jones and Ms. Underwood. Why is it more important for the clergy to understand scripture, moral reflection, Christian teaching, than for Ms. Webb to do so? Are these matters irrelevant to Ms. Webb's need to live as a Christian in the complex contemporary world in which she works?

The failure to educate laity in contemporary mainline Protestantism means, let us note this clearly, that we have fallen back into a pre-Reformation situation in which we have an almost medieval gap between an educated clergy and an uneducated laity. This is the opposite of what Luther and Calvin had in mind with "the priesthood of all believers." As with them, so now, the route to "building up the body of Christ," bringing into being the "priesthood of all believers," is by way of theological education in the church. No longer can we continue to assume that disciplined learning in matters of the Christian faith—its scriptures, teachings, language, and practices—is neither possible for nor relevant to believing Christians.

The Neighborhood Theological Seminary

In short, we are proposing that the congregation become what we call the "neighborhood theological seminary." At least three recent writers on congregational revitalization have proposed this idea, although we were the first, to our knowledge, to coin the term.[15] Richard Baxter, a

Puritan pastor in the seventeenth century, talked of the pastor as the "schoolmaster in a school," reflecting the understanding of the teaching minister that we have seen in John Calvin. Here we take a look at the proposals of these three recent authors to see what we can learn from them that promises to be helpful in our situation.

 For the first, we go back to the 1960s to Wesner Fallaw and his concept of "church education."[16] In that troublesome time for ministers, Fallaw proposed that the pastor should be the chief (not the only) teacher of the Christian faith in the congregation. He knew that Christian faith has to be learned, and that to be learned it has to be taught: "Ours is a faith to be taught, and taught with all the competency we can summon."[17] As Fallaw analyzed the situation of congregations, he discerned that one of their major difficulties arose from the fact that the various jobs of people were improperly allocated. Those with the greatest amount of theological education did the least teaching. Those who did not have a theological education and whom the church made only haphazard attempts to educate were the ones who did all the teaching. What Fallaw proposed, therefore, was a radical reassignment of the jobs in the local congregation. He suggested that everybody was working hard and getting burned out because they were all working at the wrong tasks.

Fallaw did not call for laypeople to be used less in Christian education, just for them to be *less misused*. So he called for every class in the church to be taught by the pastor! It would meet some time other than Sunday morning—during the week—and the pastor would teach it. It would meet again on Sunday morning, in a "workshop" session, and be conducted by a layperson working closely with the pastor. In this process there was a strong emphasis on the pastor as a "teacher of the teachers," empowering them for their ministry. The pastor would teach the class and the laypersons would run workshops, field trips, interest groups, and projects in the community; oversee lesson preparation, handle audiovisual aids, and so forth.

What Fallaw proposed was nothing short of making the church the schoolhouse of the Christian faith, much as the synagogue is the school of Jewish faith. He suggested an entire curriculum, breaking out of the "Bible-only" curriculum of many church curricula. The congregation would study the history of the church, Christian ethics, contemporary theology, the critical approach to the Bible, and the other religions of the world.

For its time, and in many ways still, Fallaw's approach would be welcome and helpfully transformative of much church life. Yet as we look at it from our time, we see both strengths and weaknesses. The great strength is the concept itself, that it gets serious about teaching and learning the Christian faith. Yet it raises some questions as to its adequacy for our situation today. First, it proposes a role for the pastor, as the teacher of *every* class in the church, that is probably not feasible except in churches that are quite small. In such churches, however, pastors could probably play this role well and find genuine fulfillment in it. Instead, we would propose that the pastor become the major "teacher of the teachers" of the Christian faith. Second, we would not limit the vehicles through which this task can be carried out to classes—teaching and learning should happen in all dimensions and aspects of the church's life. Third, we do not think that Fallaw's curriculum is quite the one we would propose. It is too heavily indebted to a graduate seminary model for church education. The scriptures, church history, ethics, theology, and other faiths all need to be understood; but the method of approach needs to be focused on how the lives of Christians intersect with these realities in the world of actual experience. We will return to these constructive points later. But for laypeople to be optimally functioning Christians, it would be well for them to have a grasp of the subjects on Fallaw's list. Why, for example, should they be expected to make moral decisions about complex matters when they have never been educated in Christian ethics?

 The second proposal of the "neighborhood theological seminary" as a model for contemporary congregations was ours.[18] We assume that the Christian faith must be learned, that becoming Christian does not happen "naturally" or come from participation in the culture at large. Our suggestion was that the pastor become the "overseer" whose purpose "is to nurture theological consciousness in the congregation." Nor is preaching itself a sufficient means to get this done.[19] Each congregation should develop "a program by which members are systematically and critically introduced to the major elements of the Christian faith."[20]

We proposed genuinely theological learning that is both critically ordered and disciplined and that empowers Christian people to interpret the situation in which they find themselves in the light of the Christian faith and vice versa. The goal of the effort is composed of equal parts theory and practice. It involves what is called "praxis": comprehending the vision of the Christian faith and learning the practices involved in loving both God and the neighbor. The congregation would engage in reflecting on the Christian faith in relation both to the modern and postmodern context. One of the major features of what is called "postmodernism" is a new appreciation of difference and diversity as things that are to be viewed positively rather than defensively. One implication of this is that the church is now free (as it should always have been) to view its own identity and tradition as valuable and come to grips with it as a way of shaping character and a stance from which to engage the world. We can and should appreciate our own identity as Christians and our respective denominational identities without becoming sectarian toward one another and separatist toward the world and its suffering. Previous recoveries of Christian identity have all too often been defensive and, consequently, destructive of both ecumenism and humane interfaith relationships.

The church is called into being by the gospel of Jesus Christ through the Holy Spirit to witness to the glory of God for the benefit of the world. This normative vision of the church governs our suggestion that the congregation become a neighborhood theological seminary. If the church is to bear a truthful witness both to God's glory and to the conditions for the well-being of the world, how is a congregation to get into position to do so? It can do so only through study and reflection that leads to understanding and action.

This proposal moves us farther along than did Fallaw's, while building upon it. It constructively appropriates Fallaw's vision and develops it. When calling the church a "neighborhood theological seminary," we are not saying that the local church should replicate the academic study of religion model, nontheological and value-free, in its life. Everything we do in the church teaches. Worship, liturgy, preaching, pastoral counseling and calling, administration and program development, the way people are treated, the kind of community we try to make real in the congregation—all teach the Christian faith and shape Christian character. Every group in the congregation should have study of and reflection on the Christian faith as part of its necessary agenda. Plus, teaching can be done in many ways. It should never be limited to opportunities for sermons or lectures. Nor need it be boring. Good teaching happens in all kinds of ways and is exciting and energizing. It can involve lecture, discussion, and the use of various media; take into account the arts; and occur on field trips and workshops (to name but a few ways in which teaching and learning happen).

Loren B. Mead picked up the concept of the local congregation as a neighborhood theological seminary and developed it in helpful ways. Mead suggests that the educational task of the congregation focus on the need to develop "a ministry of laypersons working in the structures of the society."[21] Congregations need to prepare people for this kind of ministry and only congregations, he suggests, can do so. Congregations are not called on to do what seminaries do—provide an educated clergy—but to "produce a different kind of minister for a different ministry." Each congregation needs to be "reinvented as a new kind of seminary—a seminary that shapes laity as effectively as seminaries of the past century shaped a professional clergy."[22]

Mead does not promise that this will be easy or quick. Nor is it a matter simply of taking what is found in seminaries and transferring that to the congregation. What is called for is, literally, reinventing new ways of developing a new kind of minister. "Members of congregations need to be challenged," says Mead, "beyond religious dilettantism to serious, long-term engagement with the stuff of the faith. Ministry in the twenty-first century is going to demand persons equipped with the biblical story and with working theologies that translate into working-world realities."[23] This means developing a full curriculum of study of the Bible, theology, history, and practical theology (which includes ethics—"practical" theology deals with what the church ought to do in various regards).

What seminaries call "field education" will be even more important in local churches. The "placements" are actual life situations—where lay ministers actually carry out their ministry. Given the state of lay theological education, remedial education will have to be undertaken (although we probably do not want to use the term) at the same time that more advanced study is provided for other members. The popularity of "Elderhostel" education programs, the fact that people will pay large amounts of money and go to considerable lengths to spend two weeks being educated in some topic, should suggest possibilities to congregations that are imaginative.

At the center of Mead's proposal is empowering laypeople to make connections between their personal theological encounters with the situations they face and the decisions they have to make, and the resources of the Christian tradition. The role of the clergy is to help make those connections, a role that requires at least as much listening as talking.

We pinpoint three mistakes that should be avoided. One is the assumption that everybody's head is stuffed full of theological knowledge and conviction; indeed, that they are absolutist, fundamentalist, and dogmatic. On this assumption, the task of theological education is to shake people awake from their dogmatic slumbers. This is the assumption that liberal theologians made, perhaps rightly, in nineteenth-century Europe. They understood their task to be making critical thinkers out of people who were overly committed to the dogmas of orthodox Protestantism. In reality, in our decidedly post-establishment, unchurched culture, people do not need more relativizing. The culture provides that in spades. What they need is to come into possession of the content of the Christian faith and to understand that faith and live it out in ways that are appropriate and pertinent.

Hence, Christian education cannot content itself with emphasizing relationality, having a good time in church, and becoming good citizens. It should teach us the Christian understanding of relationships, what Christian joy is, and how Christians can witness to and work for the common good. It should do this by helping us understand ourselves in relationship to God, Jesus Christ, the gospel, the neighbor, and the situation in which we live.

The second mistake, in our judgment, is to regard all education as bad, "hierarchical and authoritarian" as a current way of thinking has it. In this view, bad teaching happens when one person shares with another some piece of information or understanding. Good teaching, on the other hand, would educe, draw out, from the student everything the student needs to know. Sometimes this is dressed up as the "Socratic" mode of teaching. Socrates, in the early Platonic dialogues, seems to be teaching in this way; but a closer reading shows him leading his students through the basic moves of logic, which come from Socrates rather than being educed from the student.

We are as opposed to hierarchy and authoritarianism as any one else but fail to see how such opposition erases the distinction between older and younger students of the Christian faith. Older and younger students of the Christian faith are both students, hence equal, and the older should not domineer over the younger but regard them as neighbors given the older to love. But there is no Christian requirement that we disrespect those who have given their lives to understanding the Christian story and to teaching it to others. Respect for the hard work and scholarship that go into understanding has nothing hierarchical or authoritarian about it.

The third mistake is to assume that all teaching is formal, that it takes place in classrooms or classes, as does all learning. Everything in the church teaches something to somebody. When we appreciate this statement we can quickly see how any and all church occasions can be used for growth in the Christian faith. A board meeting could be briefly reminded of the nature and purpose of the church by way of framing how it goes about its deliberations. An elders' meeting could spend some time talking about the nature of ministry in the church. A fellowship dinner could be introduced with a reminder of what Christian *koinonia* is all about.

Five Steps Toward Becoming a Teaching Community

Toward the end of helping the solid content of Christian faith become the animation of *kerygma*, *koinonia*, and *diakonia*, we offer a five-step plan by which a congregation can move toward becoming a community that teaches and practices the gospel. Few congregations become vital centers of faith overnight. Most congregations mature slowly. Each gain is a small increment—sometimes barely noticeable. Slowly, however, the gains add up. We believe that the recovery of the gospel as the core of the life of the church will be the most important emphasis in the church for the next generation. Hence, our proposal is not a quick fix that a congregation, or a middle or upper judicatory, can adopt as a theme for a year, or even a quadrennium. We envision an ongoing emphasis on teaching.

If we are correct in projecting a long and intensive season in which the teaching ministry is at the center of the church's life, then patience is a crucial Christian virtue for pastors and other leaders. The long haul requires people who can work with a theme year in and year out. Such people need to have the pastoral sensitivity to know when (and how) to press the theme, and when to back off. They need to be able to celebrate the accomplishments of the teaching ministry, and they must have the resources to make their way through the inevitable setbacks, discouragements, and even hostilities that sometimes accompany wrestling with the gospel in today's challenging setting.

(1) The pastor—or other key leaders in the congregation—needs to make a decision to initiate the process to stress the teaching ministry. Those who say yes to becoming a strong teaching community need to realize that they will need to invest themselves in this process for a long time. They also need to realize that they will likely need to rearrange some of their priorities and their everyday uses of time.

Incidentally, we do not mean to imply that a single person can make a decision that rightly belongs to a representative body in a democratic church. In an optimum situation, the leaders of the congregation, and the congregation itself, should eventually make choices to emphasize the ministry of teaching and learning. In a finite world, and in a church with diminishing human and financial resources, such a decision can function as a norm that guides the congregation when it faces the hard fact of having to choose uses of its limited resources. A church that is on record as wanting to become a center of Christian teaching can ask of every potential use of time, human energy, and money, "Will this action enhance our vocation in teaching and learning the gospel and in witnessing to the gospel in concrete actions of service to the neighbor?"

However, a pastor may need several years of patient work with the leaders of the congregation, and then with the congregation itself, to reach the point at which the crucial bodies within the church are ready to make the choice to understand themselves as a teaching people.

(2) Ministers need to develop an image of themselves as teachers of the gospel. Indeed, clergy need to understand teaching as the fulcrum for

their identity. Teaching is not just one ministerial task alongside others but is central to the nature and purpose of pastoral life.

The development of this image is important because our images of ourselves determine our self-understanding, our values, and our priorities. Coming to clarity with respect to the nature and purpose of the ministry is particularly important because pastors are frequently confused about who they are and what they need to do. Ministers are often caught in a maelstrom of competing claims—teaching, leading worship, preaching, administration, pastoral calling, developing and promoting programs, therapy, evangelizing, raising funds, representing the church in the larger civic community, serving as local social conscience and prophet, and managing the church property—to name just a few. As the professionalization of the ministry has increased, the congregation, and the minister, have come to look to the minister as *the* person in the congregation to perform the ever-increasing range of responsibilities. Such a pastor is under the pressure of too many demands, especially when accompanied by an inability to sort through and decide which are more and less important. Ministers sometimes try to be all things and sometimes end up not being any of them as well as they could be. It is no wonder that burnout is a significant problem among clergy.

A clear image of who they are and what they are to do can help clergy organize their time, energy, and effectiveness. As we noted in chapter 2, in order to have the time necessary to become an insightful and fresh teacher, most pastors will need to rethink their weekly uses of time. Consistent with the biblical teaching that the Holy Spirit gives gifts for ministry to everyone in the community of faith, and with the priesthood of all believers, pastors need to pass some responsibilities to others in the community. The minister can then focus on the tasks necessary for teaching.

A teaching pastor needs to keep fresh in faith and in teaching and learning approaches. The preacher needs time for reading, continuing education, participating in disciplined clergy/colleague study groups, listening to (or viewing) tapes, engaging in conversation with others, entering into events (e.g., study and mission trips) that enlarge the pastor's range of experience, identifying what needs to be taught, imagining how to teach it creatively and reflecting. Some ministers, whose pastorates have been fragmented or fractious, may actually need to learn again how to study and think. As a part of the process of study, pastors need to be careful to interact, over time, with the broad range of concerns that are fundamental to Christian knowledge, growth, and practice.

Most congregations contain members who can be called to use their gifts for administration, for making pastoral calls, for engaging in evangelistic witness, for overseeing church property, for representing the church in the civic realm, and for other aspects of ministry. As noted earlier, we are not suggesting that clergy separate themselves from these activities altogether. The pastor needs to be in touch with such efforts in order to help educate the new leaders about their calls and responsibilities, to help coordinate the life of the community around a coherent vision, and to learn what these ministries reveal as important for the teaching ministry. But the pastor will find it counterproductive, even defeating, to add an increased emphasis on teaching to an already overloaded and under-focused routine.

When initially thinking about such a shift, the minister may not know who ought to be called to particular ministries. But over time, the process of developing a teaching community will help sort people into tasks that fit their gifts and inclinations. A part of the teaching ministry in the church may be to help people identify their gifts and calls and to prepare people for the new roles.

In the process of moving toward a more collegial approach to ministry, the congregation may encounter some disappointments. Hence, it is important for pastor and people to be committed to making a way through difficulties, to learning from them, and then to positing other approaches.

(3) Develop a long-term plan to educate the leaders of the congregation, and the congregation itself, to embrace the importance of becoming a teaching community. The minister might begin by having conversations with individuals who are formative for the church's life, then go to leadership groups, and later to the congregation at large. For instance, the pastor might spend several months visiting informally with the officers of the congregation, with the chairs of the elders and deacons (and similar leaders), and with others who—informally as well as formally—help shape the church's life. These conversations begin to create a web of shared ownership, so that the pastor is not alone in interpreting changes in ministerial and congregational practice to the congregation. As these leaders talk with others, the web grows.

Subsequently, formal presentations can be made to the leadership bodies in the church. Again, the discussions should probably take place over a long time, include a clear rationale, the practical implications, and plenty of time for questions and responses. The work of interpreting the importance of regenerating the teaching ministry (and of subsequent shifting in ministerial and lay responsibilities) should be shared by clergy and trusted lay leaders.

For optimum effect in congregational life, these bodies should take official actions in support of implementing a congregation-wide teaching emphasis. Along the way the minister and leadership may need to have a significant number of individual conversations with members who have particular questions and concerns or who have creative ideas to contribute.

The congregation as a whole then needs to become a part of the growing conversation. This phase would involve sermons, presentations at congregational meals and other functions, small group discussions, letters to the congregation, articles in church communications (newsletters, the congregation's Web page), videotapes that can be played in members' homes, and other creative modes of encouraging information and discussion. Direct conversation among pastors, congregational leaders, and the broad-based congregational membership will likely be widespread. At the conclusion of this phase—which might well last a year or two—the congregation can make a public record of its intention to orient its life in the directions we have discussed.

Such a process should encourage the church to feel a deep degree of ownership in the result. This stage will probably identify a number of people whose gifts and energies suggest that they might assume tasks that have belonged to the pastor. The process will also likely enlist gifted teachers from within the congregation.

(4) The congregation should develop a long-range plan for implementing teaching in all dimensions of its life. We cannot prescribe a formula to be followed in each congregation, because each community has qualities that are particular to it. However, in most congregations, this phase could begin with an assessment of the congregation's strengths and weaknesses in regard to Christian maturity. The plan can build on the strengths and take account of the weaknesses. Such a plan would probably include elements such as the following.

- At the heart of the plan, the preacher needs to preach teaching sermons.

- The congregation needs a comprehensive network of formal educational settings that meet people at their particular levels of maturity and that can help people grow.

- People learn in different styles and at different paces. The congregation needs to develop teaching occasions in a variety of styles of learning in order to help people find a style that takes advantage of their natural patterns of learning. Lecture, reading a book (or other resource) and talking about it, entering into an aesthetic experience, small group discussion, role play, video or audiotapes with conversation, praxis (doing something and reflecting upon it)—these are only a few styles of teaching and learning that ought to be a part of a congregation's formal program of Christian education.

■ People are available today at many different times of the day and night. Consequently, congregations need to be able to offer teaching and learning at a variety of times.

■ A cadre of teachers need to be identified and trained. Many congregations contain teachers of considerable talent who are underutilized. Such people can be put to full use. Persons who have not thought of themselves as teachers need to be raised up. All teachers need to be encouraged with training and weekly support. For instance, many congregations have found it helpful to have the pastor offer a special class for teachers. In order to be in the class, a person must be teaching, or in preparation to teach. The teachers are supported both with immediate, solid help for their teaching and with being a part of a high level of conversation concerning the Christian life.

■ The church has had graded approaches to Christian education for children and youth for generations. However, the long-established congregations have not had many graded educational materials or events for adults. The long-established denominations have assumed that adults possess basic Christian knowledge. However, this assumption is no longer reliable, even for adults who have been in the church for most of their lives. Many adults come into the church today without a prior history in the church and without any significant understanding of Christian tradition. Consequently, many of the congregations of the long-established denominations need to develop groups, educational materials, and classes for adults who want to explore Christian faith from the standpoint of beginners. These learners need basic orientation and a graduated series of materials and experiences to help them mature in Christian understanding and witness.

■ The congregational newsletter and Web page can contain significant educational materials.

■ The various groups in the life of the church need to learn how to interpret their purpose and work in terms of teaching and learning. A youth group sponsor, for instance, needs to ask, "What might a mission trip (or an afternoon at the bowling alley or anything else) teach our youth concerning the gospel, Christian community, Christian mission?"

- Group leaders need to learn to look for teaching moments in the lives of their groups—moments when the leader needs to help the group consciously interpret the group's situation in the light of the gospel. Such moments may range from celebration to prophetic critique. In a board meeting, for instance, the president of the congregation might interrupt a particularly hostile interchange in order to ask the conflicted parties, and the board as a whole, to reflect on the degree to which the manner of behavior in the conflict is appropriate in the Christian house.

This list of possibilities is only representative. Creative planning groups will discover many unmentioned elements that are needful for their situation. The key is for planners to think systematically through all phases of the life of the congregation and to discern how the community can provide opportunities for growth for all.

(5) Congregations need to develop criteria and means by which to regularly evaluate the effectiveness of the various mechanisms of congregational teaching and learning. Obvious criteria are appropriateness to the gospel, intelligibility, moral plausibility, fittingness to context, the degree to which the congregation seems to grow in faith and practice. The evaluators can create survey instruments, conduct interviews, and monitor participation. The congregation can then build on its successes and learn from its failures. The congregation also needs to regularly assess whether the teaching that is taking place community wide is sufficiently comprehensive to cover the breadth and depth of the gospel and its relationship to contemporary life.

Two cautions need to be raised in our discussion of evaluation. For one, Christian educators agree that it is notoriously difficult to gauge growth in maturity in Christian faith and life. Nonetheless, evaluators can probably get a soft indication of the degree to which the congregation's approaches are appreciated by the people and are integrated into the personal and social fabrics of the community. For another, some approaches will prove useful to a small number of people, but not to all. Congregations simply have to decide the limits of their human and material resources. If a congregation cannot help a person in the way that is best for her or him, the community may need to send that person to another congregation.

A plan to become a teaching community can help a congregation cover essential bases as it embodies teaching and learning. However, a plan and its implementation is a living organism. The plan may be modified as it is developing and being put into effect. Developing and using a plan needs itself to be the subject of continual evaluation.

Reprise

The way to return vitality to our congregations involves more than applying one or another set of techniques to congregational life in the effort to fix it. We are confident that Christian faith itself points us to the source of new life for both persons and communities. The way to congregational renewal is through the admittedly slow approach involved in returning to what always should have been the "bread and butter" of congregational life: being a challenging community of faith that stretches and empowers its members and is therefore an inviting and magnetic community. Such a community will be able to express its faith in many ways, including verbal ones. It will be a safe place, a sane asylum amid the madness of much of the contemporary world, in which issues of ultimate importance can be discussed and where we can explore what it means to live as Christians in the situation in which we find ourselves. It will be a missional community, active in hands-on ministry to the hurts of the world and deriving authentic satisfaction, deep and abiding, from that involvement. By so giving of itself, it will find itself.

4

Worship and Preaching in the Emerging Church

Not long ago, I heard the pastor of a congregation in the Reformed tradition describe a worship committee meeting that had come to a dead end. Some young people on the committee wanted to change the Sunday service to make it more "contemporary." One of them, a lifelong member of the congregation, said, "We've had exactly the same order of service my whole life. I'm bored. It's time for a change." While on vacation, another younger member of the committee had visited a congregation in which the music had a soft rock beat, the people (including the pastor) dressed in blue jeans and open collars, and the preacher used an overhead media screen to illustrate the sermon. This person commented: "That was neat. So often in our service I feel as though our worship is from the Middle Ages. But that church felt really up-to-date. That was *my* music. And I felt so natural and at home." Another member, a successful business leader, reported reading an article in a weekly newsmagazine that described several growing congregations: "The congregations in this article have video presentations, and dancers, and live drama. If we want to grow, we need to think about that." An older person sat with arms folded: "I joined this church fifty years ago because of its dignified worship and

73

its intellectual preaching. I don't like what you are proposing. And I can't believe that God would like it either."

The pastor who recounted this incident completed theological education at an East Coast divinity school in the early 1960s and reflected, "I just don't know what to think. We've always tried to do things the Reformed way, but the new ideas don't sound very much like Geneva in the sixteenth century. I have to admit that these contemporary possibilities are exciting to me, but are we going to dump four hundred years of tradition for a few measures of rock beat?"

In this chapter we take up such questions. We first offer a normative theological statement of the relationship of Christian worship and cultural context. We turn to phenomena in the contemporary climate that affect the worshiping community. How do these phenomena relate to worship and preaching? We then attempt to think theologically about the intersection of normative vision and cultural context in four approaches that characterize Christian worship today: prayer-book traditions, spirit-led communities, churches that continue the free-church tradition, and churches that have been in the free-church tradition and that now lean in the direction of combining aspects of the prayer-book and free-church approaches. We believe that it is possible for churches to take one of several different approaches to worship, so long as the approach is theologically adequate and culturally sensitive.[1]

Christian Worship in Cultural Context

Theologians of worship agree that the fundamental purpose of worship is to praise and honor God. As a contemporary servicebook, *Thankful Praise*, puts it, "The community comes together to serve God in worship."[2] Historians of worship are fond of pointing out that the basic character of worship is revealed in the etymologies of the Hebrew and Greek words for worship. In both languages, common terms for worship mean "to serve" or "to prostrate oneself." In the former case of worship as service, the ancient words are elastic in meaning. They can refer both to service offered in the liturgy and to service offered in more general life arenas. This duality of meaning points to the intimate connection between the service that is offered to God through liturgical activity and service that is offered to God through the rest of life. And the latter case, prostrating oneself before God, captures another dimension of liturgical activity: We bow before God in order to honor the divine majesty, beauty, love, and goodness.

At the same time, the service of worship is reciprocal. God acts and speaks in the service even as the community speaks and acts before God.

The worshiping body talks with God in prayer, and God responds. The church listens for God's counsel through Bible readings and preaching. In the spirit of the previous chapter, we might say that the sermon is an act of mutual critical correlation in which the preacher tries to help the congregation correlate the gospel with its current situation, even as the preacher reflects with the congregation on points at which its situation prompts the community to reassess its understanding of the gospel and the Christian tradition. At its best, preaching is an event of revelation. In the breaking of bread, God through Christ assures the people of divine love, grace, and presence. In the service of worship, as in all arenas of life, God always speaks and acts in integrity with God's own being in order to reveal God's unconditional love for the world and to call the community to respond with love for God and with acts of love and justice for one another and for the larger cosmos. At the most important level, then, the experience of worship is an end in itself. It glorifies God, and it provides an occasion for God and people to commune.

In addition, the worship has a teaching function. The service both *expresses* and *forms*. It provides the people of God with an occasion to express their deepest feelings to God. In the process, it also helps the community form its vision of God and the world. It helps the community identify ideas, actions, and feelings that are appropriate to Christian vision and those that are not. While the service as a whole is not designed to be didactic, it does teach.

Christian teaching takes place through the materials that are included and excluded in the service, through the types of liturgical actions that are permitted and forbidden, through the leadership of the service (who leads and who does not), as well as through the nature and quality of the congregation's participation. For instance, the members learn what is (or ought to be) considered normative Christian belief through the ways in which God is addressed and the things that are said about God in the prayers, in the hymns, in the Bible readings, in the sermon, in the words at the sacred table.

In the midst of the service, the sermon is often an act of overt teaching. Indeed, the two of us would like for the sermon to become more regularly, and more obviously, a distinctive moment of teaching and learning.[3] The service of worship is the largest regular gathering of the community. Through the sermon, the pastor has a marvelous opportunity to think critically with the congregation about the intersection of the Christian vision and the world.

The service of worship has a symbolic character. The words and actions of worship represent the congregation's understanding of God's relationship to all of life, as well as how the community should respond to God and neighbors (in the spheres of both humankind and nature) in the whole of life. In a sense, the experience of worship is a microcosm of our encounter with God in the macrocosm.

A caveat: All services and sermons teach through word, action, and feeling. But the *fact* that they teach does not mean that they teach what *ought* to be taught and learned among Christian people. Services of worship, even ones that are aesthetically designed and well led, can teach things that are less than Christian. For instance, a service that begins with the Pledge of Allegiance to the flag of the United States (one of us has been to such a service) confuses the nation with the Transcendent. Hence, it is imperative for the Christian community always to be evaluating the service and its constituent parts as to their theological viability.

By definition, Christian worship always takes place within particular cultures, traditions, and communities. Indeed, Christian worship needs to be fitting to the context in which it takes place in order to be intelligible in that context.

The church always employs aspects of technology in its worship. At this juncture, we are thinking of technology in both mechanical and social terms. Technology can refer to mechanical devices that affect life, such as computers, music synthesizers, and audiovisual media. It can also refer more generally to attempts to affect human attitudes and behavior by structuring human contexts according to empirically derived knowledge of human preferences as well as of psychological and sociological principles that affect human thought and action. In speaking about the technology of worship, then, we have in mind the possibility that churches could use new mechanical technologies in the service itself, such as massive screens on which to project the words to hymns, songs, and choruses. We also have in mind the possibility that worship planners could draw upon the knowledge of how people are affected psychologically and socially by particular ways of doing things.

Given the complexity of worship of the church at the turn of the millennia, it is imperative for worship planners to think carefully about the service of worship as a whole and about each element within it. The church seeks worship that in all its dimensions is appropriate to the gospel of God's unconditional love and unremitting will for justice, is intelligible, and is morally plausible. These criteria can be used to assess each part of worship.

In this respect, Christian worship finds itself in a dual relationship with its context. On the one hand, Christian worship must make use of specific cultural forms, practices, and artifacts. Whether consciously or not, the church employs some technologies in its services of worship. On the other hand, Christian worship should not become captive to the culture in which it takes place, nor should it be manipulated toward non-Christian ends through the unreflective use of technology. Susan J. White pungently describes the church's relationship with technologies.

> To the extent that worship can embody and sustain Christian love, hope, and charity, then the dehumanizing, fragmenting, death-dealing elements of technology will be called into question. To the extent that technology can enhance the sense of human freedom, the unity of the global family, and the possibility of self-transcendence, then the irrelevant, individualist, and repressive elements of worship can be called into question. In other words, if technology and worship can enter into a relationship of mutual critique, there is the possibility that both may undergo genuine renewal.[4]

A key is for the church to think critically about those aspects of technology that are appropriate to the gospel, intelligible, and morally plausible. For, as White cautions,

> The practice of Christian worship in an age dominated by technology and technological thinking is in grave danger: in danger of becoming irrelevant, and banal, in danger of becoming just another "technological fix," in danger of succumbing to the destructive values of technology, in danger of being locked into a religious or cultural ghetto, and yes, in danger of disappearing altogether.[5]

At its most insightful, Christian worship both criticizes aspects of the culture in which it takes place and draws from that culture in ways that are consistent with the gospel.

Worship points to a transcendent God who can only be known through cultural mediation but whose nature and purposes transcend any given community. No human communities, not even the best ecclesial ones, embody the divine intention perfectly.

Worship within the church may take on countercultural dimensions. By representing a universe that understands its source in a Benevolent Other and that orders itself in relationships of love and justice, Christian worship can offer an alternative vision of human and cosmic community to the prevailing practices and values of the surrounding culture. Worship leaders, in conversation with the wider Christian community, need to judge the degree to which it is apropos for Christian worship to partake of the culture and its forms and practices, and when it is necessary to cut against the grain of the culture in order to witness to the gospel of the Transcendent Other. In the process, the church needs to remember that it will never achieve a state of purity in these matters.

The Current Climate for Worship and Preaching

New cultural configurations, and fresh interpretations of the gospel and Christian tradition, prompt reflection on worship and preaching in almost every era. We identify four such phenomena that are prominent in our time. While we mention these factors individually for convenience of discussion, they interrelate. We are also aware that, for heuristic purposes, we oversimplify. Along the way, we comment on how these factors might contribute to fresh thinking about worship.

First, many people are moving from a mechanical understanding of life and the cosmos to understandings that are more organic. As a part of the Enlightenment and the Industrial Revolution, many communities began to think of the world in the image of a machine. The machine is designed to produce a product. A machine operates according to identifiable scientific laws that are expressed in propositions and that can be discussed in linear fashion. A machine is completely predictable. Each part has a specific function. When the machine is broken, a mechanic can (or ought to be able to) repair or replace the broken parts. A machine can be improved through better design and better manufacture. People become experts on different parts of the machine (and the world) and are valued in the community on the basis of their expertise.

Machinelike thinking extended to human life and to the natural world. In this view, an individual person functions much like a machine biologically, psychologically, and socially. And the community, too, operates according to identifiable scientific laws. The natural world is also viewed mechanistically. The world can be improved in much the same way that machines are improved—by redesigning or reconfiguring certain parts. Indeed, the use of machines can improve the cosmos.

The purpose of the cosmos is for its various components to perform their tasks as efficiently as possible. Individuals, communities, and nature can often be repaired or improved by the application of proper principles—medical, psychological, sociological, economic, political, or ecological.

In such a culture, worship and preaching take on something of the character of a machine.[6] To oversimplify, the liturgy is a machine that is designed to produce a product. In the process, the machine eliminates the dimension of "play," that is, interaction among various members of the community for purposes other than producing a product. The product of worship is to give glory to God and to improve human beings by meeting their needs. Insofar as many machine-age people believed that human beings are the measure of all things, the value of worship in some quarters was tied to the degree to which it yielded direct benefits to people. Further, many machine-age thinkers believed that just as a machine could be continuously improved (and even perfected), so worship could be designed to help the human community continuously improve.

Each component of the liturgy functions in a specific way. Certain parts of the liturgy (e.g., the contents of the prayers) can be exchanged from week to week. Worship leaders are experts who should know how to work the machine and its various components.

The machine-age sermon was propositional and linear. The sermon itself was a product (message) to be "delivered" in much the same way that the letter carrier delivers the mail.[7] Homiletics textbooks gave the preacher advice (based on the laws of speech and communication) on how to structure the sermon in order to achieve particular ends. Indeed, in the nineteenth century, preaching textbooks diagrammed gestures for the preacher to make in order to produce particular effects.

The machine-based understanding of life is giving way to a more organic one. Human experiences and the natural world are too variegated and bubbling to be understood in a machine model. The organic image suggests vitality, fluidity, responsiveness, interconnectedness of the various parts of the organism, creativity. An organism can creatively adapt to the environment, and some organisms can initiate change in their environmental settings. Organicism has a place for the unexpected, the novel. To be sure, the behavior of an organism often follows certain patterns that can be recognized and on which people can count. Plants, for instance, grow at relatively foreseeable rates. An organic understanding of life combines stability and the possibility of the novel.

In the organic worldview, worship and preaching become less formulaic and more biotic. Worship is less an assembly line designed to produce a product and more an experience in which the community contemplates the grace and love of God. Worship is less a means to an end and more an end itself whose primary purpose is to honor God (though, as we noted above, worship always has the effect of signaling the community as to what is apropos and what is not). The sermon is less a package to be delivered and more a moment of engagement in which preacher and congregation participate together to discern God's presence and leading. Worship leaders and preachers continue to play authoritative roles, but they do so less as authoritarian experts and more as representatives of the community with particular roles to play in guiding the priesthood of all believers.

Second, and closely related, a similar change is taking place in human patterns of receiving and processing communications. These patterns are shifting from a print orientation (with its machinelike qualities) to an audio-visual-imagistic orientation (with a more elastic, but still predictable character). Walter Ong, an eminent interpreter of the history of human interaction, describes three eras in human communication: oral-aural patterns, the alphabet and the press, and audio-visual-electronic media.[8]

Oral-aural patterns were dominant prior to the invention of the printing press and are still dominant among peoples who do not emphasize print or electronic media. In oral-aural culture, most communication takes place via the living human voice in the context of community. Memory is highly developed. Thinking is often associative and imagistic. Storytelling is a primary mode of expression. Oral-aural speech frequently has spontaneous effervescence. The person is holistically involved in the act of listening as sound waves stimulate the eardrum and create a physical resonance in the body. In oral-aural communication, all the senses are activated, and the self often feels deeply and personally involved.

The invention of the printed alphabet paved the way for literate culture, and the emergence of the printing press in the fifteenth century made print-based culture the norm in many societies. Literate culture relies upon the printed word as a primary basis for knowledge and communication. Since people can read alone, print-based culture moves in the direction of individualism. Thinking is often linear, propositional, deductive, and analytical. Knowledge is the possession of data, and the ability to explain it. Ideas become the most important expressions. Identity is articulated in clear principles. Reading stimulates the eye, which involves less actual physical movement than hearing does. It is often easier for the self to disengage from reading than from oral-aural transactions. In literate culture, oral expressions often reflect literate style; they are frequently linear, propositional, essay-like, and analytical.

Our society is moving away from a predominantly print basis to one that is shaped by the audio-visual-electronic media. The emerging era reformulates aspects of oral-aural culture in electronic format. The electronic media, which are becoming a major paradigm for human communication generally, communicate through oral-aural-visual events that stimulate the whole self. Stories and images again become primary modes of communication. Indeed, today's images involve remarkably powerful words, graphics, and music. We are told that the attention span of many contemporary persons is about five to seven minutes—about the length of a segment of a television show between commercials. Although it is possible to find in-depth thinkers on the electronic media, the sound bite has come to prominence on many airwaves as a standard genre of analysis of complex situations. But whereas communication took place face to face in oral-aural culture, it can be highly individualistic in the new world. And even when people are together for an audio-visual-electronic event (e.g., a movie), the group is often a collection of individuals singularly partaking of the event rather than a conjoined, interactive body.

Some writers claim that in order for communication in our culture to be effective, it must manifest audio-visual-electronic qualities. All communication, they say, needs to be immediate, fast-moving, imagistic, sensory, and associative, with minimal emphasis on logic, argument, and rational thought.

However, the evolving communication scene includes complications to suggest that such wholesale conversion will not be adequate for future patterns of communication. Indeed, some of these complications are reminiscent of print-based culture. The personal computer, especially when used for business, education, and personal correspondence, continues rational thinking in linear, deductive models. We have been present when a preacher with a compelling, life-related message and a warm and enthusiastic presence could hold a congregation's attention for a long time. Such speakers are more than storytellers and image makers. They also draw upon propositional thinking, logic, argument, and evidence.

Further, some communication patterns of this new era should be critically evaluated concerning the degree to which they are loving and just. Some uses of the contemporary media are manipulative. Many television commercials, for instance are designed to cause the participants to bypass genuine critical thinking on their way to the checkout counter with product in hand.

While communication patterns are shifting, our culture is not in the midst of a simple shift from thought and proposition to images and impressions. In the new era many different modes of communication are apropos. Thought, proposition, image, impression—each has a time and place for optimum use. A part of the communicator's responsibility is to determine the appropriate, intelligible, and morally plausible uses of each.

The desirability of integrating dimensions of the new communications patterns into worship and preaching is greatly debated in the church at the present time. On the one hand, the criteria of intelligibility and fitness to context suggest that worship and preaching need to consider points at which the new communication possibilities might help the liturgy and sermons articulate Christian vision in the contemporary context. On the other hand, some of the perspectives and strategies of the new technologies can subvert gospel values. Christian leaders need to think critically and creatively about how (and whether) the new technologies are appropriate to worship and preaching in a time when human patterns of perception are changing.

For instance, the evening news reduces significant world events to sound bites. The gospel and its implications for the cosmos cannot be reduced to a sound bite. However, this observation ought not necessarily and always cause the church to eschew television altogether. A congregation might use a sound bite approach in a television commercial to try to prompt the viewer to reflect on aspects of life that clamor for fuller interpretation, and it might point the viewer to a living congregation as a community of further exploration.

Many homiletics textbooks today advocate for the sermon to employ story, metaphor, image, and other poetic modes of discourse. This emphasis is timely and is consistent with many rediscoveries about the importance of these genres in human consciousness. But while an occasional sermon may be a narrative or an extended image, most sermons need also to incorporate elements of explanation, proposition, and self-conscious critical analysis. The new era does not call for an abandonment of the old, but for a homiletic that takes advantage of the best possibilities for communication.

Third, different generations of people have somewhat different life orientations and different preferences in cultural expressions, style, and taste. The most prominent generations in the church at the present time are sometimes referred to as the Builders, the Boomers, and the Gen 13ers.

The Builders are the generation who were young adults during the Great Depression and World War II. After the war, many GI Joes sought to build a world of peace and stability. They sought to accomplish this goal by building institutions (governments, businesses, homes, churches) that embodied long-term stability. A fair number of Builders think of life in the machine paradigm described above. They tend to be very hard workers and they have a strong sense of responsibility to their institutions. For many Builders, the character of life in Dwight D. Eisenhower's presidency represented their personal, social, and religious values.

Not surprisingly, many of the Builders have an institutional view of the church. One reason they value the church is that it contributes to the larger social order. While making a little joke, someone in this generation once made a revelatory remark in a board meeting when she said, "I live for these meetings." When it comes to worship and preaching, many of the builders associate reverence with quietness. They prefer services that are dignified but warm. They like repetition in ritual, though their preferences in style range from high prayer book, through Main Street worship represented by "Holy, Holy, Holy," to equally predictable but less formal revivalistic patterns. Many of them prefer music that is classical in association, and that evokes or creates some emotion. They like regularity in the service. They tend toward sermons that are linear, direct, and practical.

The Boomers were born in the baby boom of the 1950s and 1960s. Their young adulthoods were spent during the civil rights emphasis, the Vietnam war, the early years of the space program, and the deaths of John F. Kennedy, Martin Luther King, Jr., and Robert Kennedy. They expect the world always to be changing. They were the first generation to grow up with television. Their numbers, as a generation, are so large that they have always had a tremendous impact on school systems and other governmental services, marketing, and churches. Whole industries grew up to serve the Boomers. The world of their formative years combined seemingly limitless potential for social change and personal fulfillment. Whereas their parents took on tasks and supported community institutions because the older generation felt responsible for them, Boomers tend to assume responsibility for specific cultural institutions and practices only when an institution or practice interests them. However, when they get hooked, many Boomers become almost manic in their pursuit of career, sports, marriage, and family.

A Boomer friend recalls overhearing his parents on the patio at night talking about their hopes for their children and saying, "I just want them to be happy." True to the hopes of these Builder parents, Boomers are spending their lives in the quest for self-fulfillment.

In their early years, many Boomers challenged "the system" in the hope that it could be changed. They desire a large measure of control in shaping their own lives and world on the basis of values represented by Martin Luther King, Jr. and the Kennedys. When the challenge proved more difficult than anticipated, many Boomers sought other ways to change and improve the quality of their personal and social worlds while satisfying their own interests. Many of them become intensely committed to jobs, families, sports, and causes that represent their values.

In the religious realm, Wade Clark Roof characterizes the Boomers as "a generation of seekers."[9] Many Boomers are on a spiritual quest to understand the meaning of life. They seek to make sense of their worlds, and especially their changing experiences, from the perspective of ultimate reality. They want to "be happy" spiritually. Boomers follow this quest into diverse and wide-ranging religious communities ranging from traditional Christianity to Eastern religions to psychologically based groups and psychic friends. Those who are oriented to the church, or who are willing to give the church a try, are not concerned about the church as an institution for its own sake. Indeed, they are often impatient with the institutional self-centeredness and hypocrisy of the church as they remember it from the 1950s and 1960s (even though Boomers are, as a generation, quite self-centered). They are interested in how the church can help them clarify their understanding of themselves, relationships, values (and their ethical expressions), and the world. Boomers consciously seek for religion to perform its oldest and most important function: interpreting the significance of life. In order to hold a Boomer's attention, preaching needs, in a direct manner, to help make holistic sense of the bits and pieces of life from the standpoint of transcendent reality.

When it comes to modes of cultural expression, Boomers are more informal than their parents. Where their parents usually "dress up" for Sunday morning (suit, sport coat and slacks, dress, blouse and skirt), Boomers often come to worship in open collars and blue jeans. Whereas the Builders like hymns with unsyncopated meter, their children tend toward more contemporary popular music, often with a soft (or harder) rock beat. Where the Builders like long responsive readings and litanies and other formal liturgical rites that communicate stability, the Boomers prefer a more relaxed, spontaneous style of worship that allows the gathered community to be expressive. And Boomers have a proclivity for excellence in their cultural expression. When they come to worship, they want the service to manifest a high quality of leadership and "performance."

Members of Generation 13 (so named because they are the thirteenth generation in the history of the United States) were born after the baby boom and are now in their young adult years. Whereas the Boomers grew up in a world of affluence and continue to have confidence in their own potential, the formative years of Generation 13 have been a time of limitation and social breakdown. About half of the Gen 13ers grew up in one-parent homes; the subsequent pain has made many of them reluctant to make commitments.

Generation 13 is the first generation in recent memory to face the possibility of declining earning power and lower lifestyle expectations than those of their parents. They know life is difficult and the Gen 13ers do not respect people who try to make life seem easier or more optimistic than they experience it. Many of them have lost trust in public officials and in the capacity of many public institutions to sustain a just and prosperous community. Generation 13 sometimes views the drive for success and excellence in the Boomers as old-fashioned greed and self-centeredness. They are less interested in success measured against the traditional norms of career advancement, increasing income, and social mobility, and they are more interested in authenticity, relationship, and community. Boomers sometimes say of their high school children, "Never have so many young people spent so much time together doing so little." But for them, a major life purpose is to be together.

The Gen 13ers, who grew up constantly immersed in audiovisual media, value the arts—music, drama, visual modes of expression, body movement. For Generation 13, diversity is a positive value. They assume a pluralism of viewpoints on issues, and they regard multiple races, ethnicities, and life orientations to be enriching. Tolerance is, consequently, a desirable trait to many Gen 13ers.

When Gen 13ers come to church, they will take seriously a gospel that brings a realistic hope to bear on the complexities, ambiguities, and difficulties of contemporary life. They have little interest in the church as an institution; they respond positively to congregations that stress relationality and community. Some Gen 13ers avoid traditional congregations because such congregations seem emotionally and relationally empty, and because their aesthetic styles are so far removed from the audiovisual world of the Gen 13ers. Such persons frequently affiliate with newer Christian communities that eschew institutionality and are oriented to relationality. When hearing sermons, they are more persuaded by experience than by logic or argument. They prefer informal worship with lots of community participation that makes extensive use of contemporary art forms—especially contemporary music, audiovisual media, and drama.

We do not mean to overdraw the differences among generations. Ron Allen, the writer of this chapter, is 48 years old, and, hence, a Boomer by cohort. With respect to the church, however, he has more the mindset of a Builder. With five children still at home, he is increasingly understanding (if not comfortable with) the lifestyle of the Gen 13ers. Some Builders are genuinely at home in churches whose approaches to worship have been conscientiously fashioned to appeal to Boomers. Although a Gen 13er may be innately more comfortable with sermons that make extensive use of stories, I have seen Gen 13ers follow tightly reasoned arguments quite closely when the arguments have been presented with passion and luminosity. These cases remind us always to respect the fact that people are not merely exemplifications of cohorts but are individuals who are often quite complicated in their makeup and tastes.

Nonetheless, the differences in preference among the generations in worship and preaching, and in church life generally, creates a knotty problem for the Christian community. On the one hand, it is easy for Christians to segregate into generational cohorts. Thus, the 11:00 a.m. service may be in the Builder mode while the 9:30 a.m. service may be in a Boomer mode, with the Thursday evening service really for Gen 13ers. Some congregations self-consciously, or by happenstance, appeal to one group or another. Such divisions help the church think creatively about how to make use of the preferences of particular generations in the service of the gospel.

On the other hand, segregating Christians by age can work against the oneness of the Body of Christ. As Paul makes clear (Galatians 3:28), the church is to be a community in which the conventional separations of the human family are transcended. The church is to be a witness to God's intention for all persons to be joined together in a community of love, grace, understanding, mutual support, and encouragement. Such a church is a representative of the nature of human community in the coming rule of God. By contrast, a church that segments itself by generation (or by race, class, education, gender orientation, or any other conventional line of demarcation) is a mirror of the current fragmentation of the world.

We do not have a foolproof answer to this problem. Here and there, we encounter a small group in the church (a Sunday school class, a fellowship group, a team that made a mission trip together) in which the multiple generations have been mixed successfully. Such groups are living embodiments of the new community. But they seem to come about less by initiating theological conviction and more by some happenstance—congenial personalities, common interest in a project, accidentally finding themselves thrown together and then discovering that they like each other. By referring to the evolution of such communities as happenstance, we do not mean to diminish the grace evident in such circumstances. We only wish that it could be more easily and obviously brought to life in other situations. We suspect that difficulties in the relationship of different cohorts in the church is a manifestation of sin with which the Christian community will simply have to live until the eschaton. In the meantime, however, the church needs to keep before its consciousness the tension between its present reality and its visionary ideal.

Fourth, services of worship in some European American congregations of the long-established denominations are lethargic. Our impression (based on worshiping as guest preachers with many different congregations of the aforementioned denominations, particularly in the Middle West) is that many services feel tired. Much of the music is dirge-like. The service drags. The worship leaders and the participants give little evidence of passion or conviction. The congregation does not seem to have a lot of energy for singing, for participating in the responsive readings, or for otherwise indicating that they are involved in the service. The events of worship appear to be automatic, without a vivid animating spirit. Indeed, the ennui of the service is sometimes such that we are grateful when the benediction is pronounced. To summarize: Some services are lifeless and boring.

This lethargic quality is not directly correlated with the style of the service. We sometimes feel it in congregations with formal prayer-book practices (such as Episcopalian, Lutheran, and Roman Catholic communities). We sometimes sense it in churches that have maintained the free church tradition (such as the various Baptist bodies). We most often feel lethargy in communities whose liturgical lives combine elements of the prayer-book heritage with impulses from the free churches (such as the Christian Church [Disciples of Christ], the Presbyterian Church [USA], The United Methodist Church, and the United Church of Christ). Our personal experience with the spirit-led churches is limited, but neither of us has ever been in such a congregation whose worship is lethargic.

We hasten to add that lethargy is not the universal tone of the worship life of congregations in these communities. The services of communities across the liturgical spectrum can be engaging. Liturgical expression that consists mostly of reading (e.g., Episcopalian worship) can be as powerful and engaging as spirit-led worship.

What are the differences between services of worship that are lethargic and services that seem to have vitality? Our impression is that two factors are paramount. (1) The skill of the worship leaders plays an important role. Careful preparation, speaking loudly enough so as to be heard in every nook and cranny of the sanctuary, speaking with feeling and energy, moving at the right time and with purpose and direction, having a sense of when to honor silence—such traits work together to help the service manifest vitality. (2) But a further factor is more important: The root of vital worship is the awareness of the presence of the living God. When carefully reflected upon, this awareness gives rise to theological clarity, to the connection of the service to the lives of the members of the worshiping community and to their larger social settings, and to a palpable sense of conviction on the part of the leaders and the congregation. In the service, the people talk clearly and passionately about the awareness of the holy and about how it critically informs their worlds.

Any approach to liturgy can become a vehicle for vital Christian worship when it is powered by these latter qualities. Spirit-led congregations are perhaps most dramatic in their recognition of the divine leading.

However, the feeling of the sacred can permeate a prayer-book service with equal, if less dramatic, intensity. The perception of the divine presence can become the spark that moves a service from a fine technical performance into a sacramental experience. A worshipful response to the knowledge of God can transform the most liturgically disjointed service into a moment of awe and wonder.

Hence, in our judgment, the *primary antidote to lethargy in worship is theological revitalization.* To be sure, worship itself can play a role in theological regeneration, for worship helps form the congregation's awareness of God. And worship planners need to develop services that fittingly bring their traditions into a new day. *But the key to the renewal of worship has to do less with creativity in worship format and more with renewing the theological heart of the church.* Thus, a church with a lethargic liturgy might well begin the path to vitalization by invigorating the teaching of the gospel throughout the congregation's life system.

These conclusions are supported by a field study made by our colleague Keith Watkins. Watkins visited two congregations in Louisville, Kentucky, that are quite different in heritage and yet are each quite vital centers of worship. Each has recovered the power of its own tradition while reformulating aspects of that tradition in "compelling cultural forms" for our time.

In the early 1980s, the Roman Catholic Cathedral of the Assumption appeared to be a dying downtown congregation whose Sunday services were attended by a handful of people. Today, the congregation is flourishing. The change resulted from a complex of factors that included expanded teaching, developing mission projects for the hungry and homeless in the downtown area, and conscientiously inviting and welcoming newcomers into the community. Worship was a key part of the revitalization. The worship space itself was simplified and redecorated. The rites, of course, are contemporary Roman Catholic; they are led with energy and feeling.

 The music combines classical and contemporary and is led with energy. Watkins reports, "My overall sense was delight in being part of this service. The beauty of the church, the integrity of the service, the stateliness of the ceremonies, and the robust piety of the music drew me in. The emphasis upon worship and the minimizing of organizational matters struck me in a highly positive way."[10]

Southeast Christian Church is a part of the Christian Churches and Churches of Christ affiliated with the North American Christian Convention. In heritage this movement is a cousin to the Christian Church (Disciples of Christ). Watkins describes the order of the service at Southeast as "virtually identical to that in most congregations of the Christian

Churches and Churches of Christ." The free church service begins with praise and prayer, moves to Bible reading and the Lord's supper and offering, with the sermon following, and an invitation to discipleship as the last element. The Lord's supper is conducted in a very simple way. A lay elder presides at the table and makes a brief interpretation of the significance of the Supper as assuring the community of God's redeeming work through Christ. The same elder then offers a free, full prayer as blessing over the bread, the cup, and the experience of partaking. The music is "highly eclectic," comprising traditional hymns, gospel songs (in both the Fanny Crosby and contemporary veins), and scripture choruses. The words to the hymns, songs, and choruses are printed in the bulletin and are also projected on an attractively designed overhead screen. Accompaniment varies with the style of the piece: traditional organ, traditional or contemporary piano, wind ensemble. The bulletin is plain. Except for reading a passage from the Bible in unison, and singing, the congregation does not participate verbally a great deal in the service. While Watkins has his "own disagreements" with the liturgical system at Southeast, he is impressed with the profound religious character of the service. He concludes,

> My strongest impression of this service is that it is fully consistent with the essential character of the liturgical tradition which it represents. The leaders of this congregation have reinvigorated a traditional form, given it a strong musical quality, and developed a highly accomplished mode of presentation.[11]

These conclusions suggest that few congregations need to start from scratch about how to move toward vital worship. A congregation seeking renewal in worship might begin by recollecting the strengths of its tradition and then by identifying points at which its tradition might be informed by enlivening cultural forms and practices. We make some general suggestions in these regards in the next part of the chapter.

Four Traditions of Worship

In the Euro-American sectors of the United States and Canada, worship takes place not only within culture, but in specific traditions of worship within culture and within the Christian house. Over the last 400 years, four major approaches (with innumerable subthemes) have developed in Christian worship in the West. As noted earlier, these are the prayer-book tradition, the spirit-led communities, churches that have considerable freedom in the development of their worship but that currently lean in the direction of the prayer-book traditions, and the free churches that continue in the pattern of freely developing their worship. We now evaluate these patterns and consider how the perspectives discussed earlier in the chapter might intersect with each family of worship.

The *prayer-book (or worship-book) traditions* are represented by Episcopalian and Lutheran bodies. The service of worship is drawn from a book that sets the liturgy and that provides the Bible readings and the wording for the major prayers and other components of the liturgy for the day. Typically, the style of the service is rather formal. In carefully defined elements, the service moves from an opening through the Bible readings and sermon. These are followed by the long prayers (often with the congregation voicing persons or situations for which to pray) and the creed. The service, in its fullness, is designed to conclude with the eucharist. The minister creates the sermon afresh each week. The service usually has opportunities for the pastor and the congregation to add to the prayers from events and experiences in the contemporary world and to contribute in other limited ways to the service. Prayer-book services often take place in highly symbolic worship spaces, with symbolic dress and ritual movements. Usually, these congregations follow the Christian year and a lectionary. The most common table of readings in use in Protestant churches in North America is the Revised Common Lectionary.

The theological content infusing prayer-book liturgies is typically appropriate to the gospel, intelligible, and morally plausible. The worship in such congregations changes from time to time. For example, the language of the liturgy is no longer King James English, but has been made contemporary. Materials in the new worship books take account of personal and social phenomena that are prominent when the books are prepared; some of these phenomena remain "current" during the life of the prayer book, while others fade quickly from the scene. The prayer-book churches make minimal use of electronic audiovisual technology. The music is often traditional. Even the contemporary music that makes its way into prayer-book services is often reserved and reminiscent of older music with its traditional meter.

Services of worship in the Roman Catholic Church are also in the prayer-book tradition. But over the last thirty years Roman Catholic worship in many parishes has become somewhat informal. Such services follow the prescribed liturgy and the assigned prayers, but worship leaders are quite relaxed. Contemporary music is frequent, often with a soft rock beat and accompanied by instrumental groups. The Roman Catholic Church has also experienced a rebirth of interest and quality in preaching.

The prayer-book tradition has many strengths. The materials in the worship books are often of high theological and aesthetic quality. While the primary end of the service of worship is to honor God, a secondary result of worship is that the congregation learns through the liturgy who God is, what God offers, and how God expects the cosmic community to live. The liturgy often evokes an almost mystical awareness of God. The predictability of the liturgy communicates assurance in a world of rapid change and a world that sometimes seems confusing, chaotic, and even threatening. The regularity of the liturgy from week to week communicates a vision of God and Christian community that is stable and trustworthy. The symbolism of worship space, dress, and ritual action is often quite beautiful.

The approach to worship in the prayer-book tradition is rooted in the third and fourth centuries of the Common Era. Hence, congregations who worship in this way often have a deep sense of being a part of the communion of saints that transcends time and space. The connection to earlier generations of Christians appeals to a fair number of Boomers and Gen 13ers, who have been brought up with such a permeating focus on the present moment that they are starved to feel a part of a community with a sense of roots and history. The prayer-book churches could draw more overtly on this quality in their public statements, especially in advertising and other modes of inviting people to explore the world of the gospel through their venue. And since the prayer-book traditions are found worldwide, Christians who use them often have a vivid sense of the global ecumenicity of the church. This quality, too, should be highlighted as a potential draw to the increasing number of persons who feel a growing connectedness of the whole world.

In these latter respects, the prayer-book liturgy has a countercultural quality. In the midst of the United States with its lionization (even idolization) of individualism, consumerism, immediate gratification, and narcissism, the prayer-book tradition evokes another world: communal, historical, in the embrace of a gracious, benevolent, trustworthy Other whose love and call bestow identity and purpose to transcend our individual moments with their heights and depths. Many Boomers and Gen 13ers are interested in alternatives to present lifestyles. The prayer-book churches could more visibly offer their approach to worship as such an alternative.

But the prayer-book approaches also have liabilities. The prayer books are slow to change in response to new developments in the cosmos. A worship book enshrines theology and language that may be immensely formative and expressive at a particular moment in history, but that seems dated long before the life of the particular version of the prayer-book has ended. Prayer books need to be updated frequently. The prayer-book approach in itself seems quaint and antique. Repetition from week to week and year to year can become dull, especially if the services are not led with vigor. Consequently, planners and leaders of worship need to work to be fresh and to express their conviction for the gospel in the way they lead worship. And we have noticed that occasional leaders and congregations in the prayer-book traditions regard their approach to worship as The True One; some of them have an inflated sense of their own importance. People who love the prayer-book tradition can commend it with a sense of humility.

At the other end of the spectrum, in the *spirit-led churches* the services of worship can be quite different from week to week. The congregations that most fully embody this approach believe that the free movement of the Holy Spirit leads the gathered community in worship. The churches in this tradition are represented by the various Pentecostal and charismatic bodies (e.g., the Assemblies of God) and the unprogrammed worship of the Society of Friends. Many African American Christian communities worship in this vein. To be sure, the worship of these churches usually follows a pattern from one week to another. But within the pattern spontaneity is often evident. Individuals or groups may feel prompted to contribute to the service on the spur of the moment. For instance, someone may feel led to sing a solo or to lead the congregation in a chorus, or to speak in tongues, or to interpret prophecy, or to celebrate some mighty act of God, or to confront the people with a shortcoming. On a larger scale, the order of the service may be rearranged even as the service is taking place. Indeed, I have even been present when the service developed without a sermon (even though the pastor was fully prepared to preach).

In the charismatic congregations, exuberance is often electric. A congregant can "feel something" just by walking into the worship space. The music is often very contemporary, accompanied by rock-type instruments. The hymnbook has frequently disappeared from the worship space in favor of the projection of words on an overhead screen. Many of these churches make extensive use of electronic audiovisual media. The preacher freely selects a passage from the Bible as the basis for the sermon and sometimes moves seriatim through whole books of the Bible from week to week. These churches have long had members of all ages, but in the last quarter of the twentieth century they have become particularly appealing to Boomers and Gen 13ers.

This approach to worship has several positive qualities. These services are often animated by a pronounced awareness of the divine presence. The worship of the radically free churches attempts to be immediately responsive to that presence. The service can also be impressively contemporary as the liturgy itself can account at once for events that are occurring in the congregation and in the larger culture. These congregations often make highly sophisticated use of audiovisual-electronic technology; the service of worship seems very "up-to-date" and people experience continuities between the technology of worship and the technology of the rest of their world.

People often feel a tremendous and empowering sense of freedom in the very act of worship, a freedom that they do not feel in any other arena of contemporary life. Henry Mitchell comments on this aspect of the worship from the perspective of the African American community.

> Shouting may at times be put on or manipulated. But at its best, it *teaches* "Aunt Jane" and all the rest that the presence of God is sheer ecstasy—that before God we can be absolutely free and uninhibited—and that God freely accepts and loves the real person that we have to hide almost everywhere else. The ecstasy of being somebody-to-the-hilt for even five minutes *teaches* enough faith to keep an oppressed and despised Black man courageous and creative for another week.[12]

The service also brings the priesthood of all believers to a remarkably noticeable expression as the participation of members in the service makes the worshipers active priests for one another in dramatic ways.

This approach to worship also has limitations. It can become so focused on immediate experience that worshipers lose sight of the importance of understanding that experience in the light of central theological affirmations and norms and from the larger, historically informed, Christian community. While this approach to worship symbolizes God's immediacy and energy, the vision of God that is implied in the spontaneity of the service does not always communicate a sense of divine predictability and pattern. Furthermore, the communities that worship in this tradition do not always have evident norms by which to evaluate the service and the things that happen in it. Can the community always be *certain* that things said in the name of the prompting of the Holy Spirit reflect that source? The writer of 1 John was so aware of distortions in the gospel that can result from human finitude as to say, "Beloved, do not believe every spirit, but test the spirits to see whether they are from God; for many false prophets have gone out into the world" (1 John 4:1). Worship leaders in this tradition need constantly to be reflecting critically on what is taking place during the service in the light of the criteria of appropriateness, intelligibility, and moral plausibility.

As a further limitation, the experience of ecstasy is so consuming that it can become an end in itself. Pastors and other leaders in the community need to make it clear that ecstasy is intended to empower mission. Further, some persons seem to rely upon immediate experiential awareness to indicate the divine presence and leading; a few others go one step further and suggest that one must demonstrate signs of ecstasy (e.g., speaking in tongues) as proofs of God's presence and activity in one's life. Preachers and teachers in these communities need to help the members recognize that God's providential power and presence are not dependent upon their immediate feeling; the congregation needs to learn how to be aware of God even when they do not have immediate personal cognizance. And the dramatic technology can be so mesmerizing that it becomes an end in itself.

Only a generation ago, scholars could speak of three movements in Christian worship: the prayer-book tradition, the spirit-led tradition, and a middle ground in which worship was predictably (though not invariably) structured and in which many worship materials were developed afresh from week to week. During the middle years of this century, this middle-ground approach to worship was characteristic of many congregations of the Methodists, Presbyterians, Baptists, Christian Churches, Churches of Christ, and Christian Church (Disciples of Christ).

In the last generation, however, this broad middle movement has subdivided into two venues with different emphases. Congregations from across the denominational spectrum can be found in each subdivision, though some patterns of denominational association have developed. Some congregations continue in *the traditional free-church approach*. This approach is typically found among the various Baptist bodies, the Nazarene and Wesleyan churches, the Christian Churches and Churches of Christ, the Church of God (Anderson, Indiana), and the independent community and Bible churches. Other congregations, under the impulse of a historically rooted liturgical renewal movement, lean toward the prayer-book tradition while continuing to prepare elements of the service afresh each week. This latter approach tends to be embraced by congregations of The United Methodist Church, the Presbyterian Church (USA), the United Church of Christ, and the Christian Church (Disciples of Christ).

In the *traditional free-church approach*, like that of Southeast Christian Church described above, the service begins with a call to worship and a hymn of praise and moves through Bible readings, a pastoral prayer, music, and an offering, with the sermon coming at the conclusion. The Christian Churches and Churches of Christ typically include a simple observation of the Lord's supper, often prior to the sermon. The prayers are composed each week by the pastors and the lay leaders. The congregation vocally participates in the service mainly through singing, a unison Bible reading, and an occasional responsive reading or litany. Audiovisual-electronic technology is often employed extensively.

The seeker service, a manifestation of the free approach, deserves special comment.[13] As its name implies, the seeker service is designed for seekers, for persons who are on a quest (consciously or unconsciously) to understand the meaning of life. Church leaders do not typically intend the seeker service to be full-bodied Christian worship. Planners envision the service as an evangelistic witness—a means to offer the gospel in an inviting and comfortable format to seekers. The elements of the service are designed to show how the gospel promises a positive perspective within which to understand life.

Seeker services attempt to create an atmosphere in which the unchurched can feel culturally comfortable, and unthreatened by traditional Christian modes of expression. Such services tend to be quite informal. They employ formats and technologies that have not been typical in recent Christian worship: live drama, electronic media presentations on giant television screens, body movement, dance, readings of poetry and other modes of literature, personal testimonials. Some seeker services contain a sermon in which the pastor relates Christian faith to some aspect of contemporary life, usually speaking in categories of thought from the everyday worlds of the listeners, and drawing little on traditional theological language. Each element of the service aims to relate the gospel to the everyday lives of seekers. Some churches have built worship spaces specifically for the seeker service. Often this space contains very few traditional Christian symbols and is often more like an auditorium than a "sanctuary."

Seeker services can certainly make a witness that is appropriate to the gospel, intelligible, and morally plausible. Seeker services are a creative experiment in evangelism at the turn of the millennium. Their purpose is to spark interest in the Christian world. They have had considerable success in helping persons (especially Boomers) who grew up in the church but who drifted away become reacquainted with Christian faith. They have been somewhat effective in introducing the possibility of Christian faith to persons who have not been a part of the Christian community. However, as persons grow in Christian maturity, the seeker service is not a substitute for full-bodied Christian worship.

A church with a carefully thought-out seeker service usually has a service at another time for those who understand themselves as Christians. As persons become interested in Christian faith and life, the congregation's leaders encourage them to grow by participating in learning events and in the more complete experience of worship. For instance, the most famous congregation to employ the seeker service, the Willow Creek Community Church in suburban Chicago, has a vast network of small groups in which persons can grow in Christian faith, as well as services of worship that draw upon the fullness of Christian doctrine.

Some congregations use the "contemporary service" as a variation on the traditional free-church approach. Such services try to embody seasoned Christian worship through thoroughly contemporary music and other forms, such as live drama, electronic media presentations, body movement, dance, and readings of contemporary literature. The sermon helps the congregation come to grips with the contemporary implications of traditional Christian texts, themes, and language.

Many congregations now offer both traditional and contemporary services. This approach has both positive and negative qualities. On the positive side, multiple services in different styles maximize a congregation's attempt to serve persons who respond to different approaches to worship. To oversimplify, many Builders tend to like traditional services, while a fair number of Boomers and Gen 13ers are drawn to contemporary services. The contemporary service can feel contemporary. In the committee meeting that we reported at the beginning of the chapter, one of the people who had attended such a service said, "That church felt really up-to-date. That was my music. And I felt so natural and at home." On the negative side, the presence of multiple services can have the effect of creating separate and unrelated communities within the same congregation. Congregational leadership needs to encourage the different groups to realize their oneness in the body of Christ. Further, contemporary services can so focus upon the "now" that they lose the historical memory of Christian tradition. Without a sense of history, a church can become a theological orphan, left with nothing more than its own immediate resources for worship, faith, and life. Communities with no historical memory are especially susceptible to repeating errors from earlier in the church's life.

The traditional free-church approach to worship brings together warmth, simplicity, and dignity with a touch of informality. As such, they are often continuous with central qualities of middle-class life in Euro-America. This mode, with its emphasis on responsiveness to the preferences of local communities, is very much in tune with the democratic spirit. Such services can be elegant as they help the community to acknowledge the presence and work of God and to reflect on the life of the world in Transcendent perspective. The predictability of the service suggests

trustworthiness in God; the adaptability of the service suggests God's responsive character. The structure and style of the service can easily accommodate
new elements and new ways of doing familiar things. Such services can often
bring the traditional and the contemporary into friendly communion.

The traditional free approach is also susceptible to abuses. Worship
leaders do not always plan carefully. Worship materials and moments sometimes appear to be composed on the spot. Without the benefit of prior
reflection or planning, such occasions can be shallow, and even repetitive
from week to week, as people mouth the same platitudes. Consequently,
worship leaders need to plan creatively and carefully for each part of the
service, even as they recognize that they may alter the plan of worship in
response to developments that unfold in the service itself. The openness
of this style of worship to middle-class lifestyle and the democratic spirit
can also lead to a danger. It is especially easy for this service to lose its
transcendent frame of reference and its prophetic power as it becomes a
celebration of the current *zeitgeist*. At its worst, such worship can become
idolatrous as it confuses God with temporal realities, such as the state, or
limited notions of human community. Consequently, the worship leaders
need always to be evaluating the service and its parts as to their appropriateness, intelligibility, and moral plausibility. Further, unless a community
actively cultivates a memory of the history and norms of Christian worship, a local congregation can measure the quality of worship against
nothing more than its own preferences and feelings. The result can be
patterns of worship that are idiosyncratic and even sub-Christian. Worship planners can help the congregation keep in touch with the larger
world of Christian thought and practice.

Another approach *leans toward the prayer-book tradition while continuing
to prepare elements of the service afresh each week*. This approach has become
widespread in the last generation among congregations that formerly
moved in the traditional free-church approach (e.g., The United Methodist Church, the Presbyterian Church [USA], the United Church of
Christ, and the Christian Church [Disciples of Christ]). It combines aspects of the theology and structure of the prayer-book traditions with the
free composition of many of the elements of the liturgy.

This approach came about for two reasons. First, the liturgical renewal spurred by Vatican II led liturgical scholars and ministers in these
churches to rediscover the prayer-book traditions, their historic roots (especially in the liturgy identified with Hippolytus), and their considerable
strengths. Second, in the 1960s and 1970s, much of the worship of the
churches just named was lethargic and in need of reinvigoration. The
prayer-book approach offers forms that have a capacity, demonstrated across

centuries, to carry the church from one generation to another. While adapting to the prayer-book tradition, the churches in this domain seek to retain (and even enhance) a great strength of traditional free church worship—its occasional character.

The services in this approach tend to manifest the structure of the prayer-book liturgies. After a liturgical gathering of the community with call to worship, prayer, and singing, the first part of the service recalls God's initiatives in behalf of the world, especially as interpreted through Bible readings and preaching. The community responds to God's initiatives through affirmation of faith, prayer, and offering. In its complete form, the service climaxes in the Lord's supper with the assurance of God's presence and redemptive purposes. When the Lord's supper is celebrated, many congregations use a rather full version of the Great Thanksgiving that includes a preface, a sanctus, words of institution, a memorial, and an epiclesis. This service tends to be somewhat formal in character. The service often incorporates a wide variety of hymns, songs, and choruses, with some emphasis on music from other cultures.

This approach brings together many of the strengths and weaknesses of both the prayer-book tradition and the traditional free church as already discussed. In addition, we notice difficulties with the practice of this approach as it is adopted by churches that have been freer in their worship. The worship leaders, especially clergy, sometimes seem stiff and self-important. The services can contain so much congregational reading that this aspect of congregational participation becomes anesthetic. (Recently, for instance, one of us was at an ordination service in this mode for which the worship bulletin was thirteen pages long—most of it in the form of responsive or unison readings.) Members who remember the simpler, freer style of worship sometimes speak nostalgically of those days.

Such difficulties are not inherent; they seem to result from congregations shifting from one mode of worship to another and not being quite comfortable with the new mode. This approach can be fueled by theology that is appropriate, intelligible, and moral. And this approach is generating a lot of excitement, but it is yet to be seen if it can become the soul of the worship of the churches that have turned to it in the last decades.

Conclusion

One of us once heard a sermon entitled "Any Old Bush Will Do." The preacher's point is that God can use "any old bush" to speak to us as God spoke to Moses at the burning bush. Much the same is true of worship. Any intelligible form will do, as long as it is charged with appropriate theological content and is led with passion befitting the living God.

5

Christian *Koinonia*—More than Animal Warmth

In western Nebraska, when a blizzard knifes across the open plains, cattle huddle together to keep warm. Even when the howl of the wind is loudest, the rancher can still hear the cattle calling to one another as they press their bodies together against the cold and the wet.

People, too, seek animal warmth. We huddle together against the cold of contemporary life. A cocktail party, for instance, can be such an occasion. A room filled with people. Candles aglow. Crackers and cheeses on the table. People talking easily. Laughter running like an undercurrent through the room, bubbling up in one group and then another. A good cocktail party is genial, and it provides a welcome measure of human contact and release, especially for those who work and live in relative isolation and tension.

Christian *koinonia*, however, is more than animal warmth. *Koinonia* is a transliteration of a Greek word that is sometimes rendered "fellowship." The word fellowship has lost favor in recent years for two reasons. For one reason, the term "fellow" sometimes refers to males, as in the song, "For He's a Jolly Good Fellow." Hence, the designation "fellowship" is said to reinforce patriarchy. For another reason, "fellowship" as commonly used in the church has come to have bland associations. The "fellowship hall," for instance is often a room whose decor is innocuous: pasty green walls, the floor covered with a litter of stray tiles, a dim stage, religious pictures from the 1930s hung randomly on the walls.

Over the last generation, quite a few congregations have discovered koinonia as a replacement term. So, many congregations have the Koinonia Class, the Koinonia Room, the Koinonia Khoir (yes), and the Koinonia Retreat. Many in the church seem instinctively to sense that koinonia evokes more theological power than current associations with fellowship. However, the church seldom explicitly identifies the fullness of meaning that is implied in the ancient notion of koinonia. Indeed, at times, the church settles for animal warmth, when it really needs to encourage koinonia.

In this chapter we first probe the biblical and theological roots of koinonia. We then consider changing patterns of koinonia in the church. We focus on small groups and larger group settings as expressions of koinonia that are promising for the emerging church. The chapter concludes by relating the koinonia of the congregation to that of the wider church and world.

Biblical Roots of Koinonia

The designation koinonia makes its way into the Bible from the world of Greek thought and practice. The First Testament does not have a word that is precisely parallel to the Greek term koinonia. In fact, the word *koinonia*, and its cognates, is found only a few times in the Septuagint (the Greek translation of the First Testament) and a few times in extrabiblical literature prior to the first century C.E.

However, koinonia shares much in common with fundamental perspectives on community in the First Testament. Both the *koinonia* word family and the Jewish literature of antiquity envision human identity as communal. Human beings are not individual units who exist independently of one another. A community is more than a collection of individuals who exist in the same space. The identity of the community to which the human being belongs is integral to the identity of the individual, and the individual is, warp and woof, a part of the community. As noted in chapter 2, scholars often describe this phenomenon as corporate identity. All individuals in a community are interconnected. An individual embodies the community, and the community is represented in the individual. The joy of the community is that of the individual, and the individual shares in the people's sufferings and sorrows. Many of the psalms, for instance, use the representative "I" in which the first person singular pronoun speaks collectively for the psalmist and for many others who find themselves in a similar situation. The notion of corporate identity, however, does not absolve the self from responsibility for her or his own actions; individuals must still accept the consequences for violations of community mores. In the world of corporate identity, individual violations of the common life are understood to affect the community as a whole. And the people could be blessed and cursed as a whole.

The Hebrew idea of covenantal community is central to this notion. The various covenants in Hebrew history are communal in character. God cuts covenant with the Hebrew people as a body. As a part of the covenant with God, the people are joined together in covenantal relationship with one another. The forms and regulations for communal life (e.g., the rites in the tabernacle and temple, the commandments) are designed to implement the practical implications of covenantal community. The people are joined together in obligation to God and to one another. By virtue of the community's commitment to God, the people are interconnected. Their lives are joined together. When the people practice injustice (i.e., when they violate the responsibilities necessary to provide in an optimum way for all among them), the community breaks down. In the worst instance, they suffer economic and social collapse. When the people practice justice (e.g., when they demonstrate their interconnectedness by living out the responsibilities of the covenant for one another), the community is strong and vital.

The synoptic Jesus beautifully summarizes Jewish perspective on these matters when he summarizes the law in two commandments. The community is to love God with heart, soul, mind, and strength, and is to love its neighbor as itself (Mark 12:28–34 and parallels). Love for God and love for neighbor are interconnected. One way the community embodies its love for God is through neighbor-love. Acts of love for the neighbor are expressions of love for God.

Although the primary background of koinonia is in Greek practice and philosophy, its emphases are congenial to the communal dimensions of Hebrew identity. The notion of koinonia becomes a significant description of the nature of the church. Though private possession of land and other possessions remained the usual practice in Greek history, several Greek philosophers envisioned common ownership (*koinos*) of possessions as the ideal form of social organization.[1] Plato believed that individual self-centeredness, and particularly private ownership, was an enemy of the common good; he encouraged individuals to be responsible for the state. He exhorted the guardians of the state, and the soldiers, to divest themselves of private goods. They should be fed, clothed, and housed from the public store. They would then be freed from the corrupting desire for gain. In the model world, the land should be regarded as common possession. The people would be allotted equal plots for farming and ranching, and the plots could not be sold or otherwise divided or amassed. The ideal state has no need of silver or gold. Indeed, money corrupts.

Aristotle acknowledges the usefulness of some private possession because communal ownership "leads to neglect." However, all citizens should have the goods and resources necessary for subsistence. Aristotle called for usufruct—the custom by which people have a right to the use of the property of others. According to the Cynics, nature is the basis of the common life: The things of this world have been created for the use of all. "The Cynic, who is a friend of God, draws the conclusion that among friends, all things are common." Stoicism, while not renouncing private ownership, regards the human race as sisters and brothers who have access to the world's goods much like the members of a family.

Some groups in the ancient world practiced communitarianism. For instance, Pythagoras and his disciples left their families, renounced private ownership, and placed their resources at the service of Pythagorean community. The Jewish people provide a famous example. The Essenes, whose most famous community was located on the edge of the Dead Sea at Qumran, are described by both Josephus and Philo as practicing communal ownership. Indeed, the Dead Sea scrolls use the phrase "poor in spirit" for those who voluntarily divest themselves of their goods and turn them over for the common use of the community. The community then lives out of the common body of money and other possessions.

The term *koinonia* echoes this communitarian background. A *koinonos* can be a participant or a business partner. In Luke, for instance, James and John are partners in the fishing business (Luke 5:10). Koinonia can refer to close association with others. Married life can be a koinonia (Malachi 2:14, 3 Maccabees 4:6). Koinonia is powerful: a koinonial relationship shapes the character and behavior of those involved. Consequently, the apocryphal book of Sirach asserts that whoever has koinonia with the proud becomes like them (Sirach 13:1–2). The book of Wisdom states that wisdom ought have no koinonia with envy (Wisdom 6:23).

More specifically, a koinonia could be a community of persons who participate together on the basis of their common bonds. In a koinonia, people regard one another as partners. Indeed, in the commercial world, a koinonia is a legal partnership. Among the ancients, however, the emphasis in a commercial koinonia is less upon the legal obligations of the partners than upon the moral responsibilities for one another. The partnership is a shade of the common bond presumed by the philosophers.

J. Paul Sampley argued that by the time of the early church, a koinonia could be a community established and regulated by a social contract. A koinonia could be created by a mandate, by the sale of something or someone, by hire for a temporary period of time, or by voluntary association. According to Sampley, a koinonia could be created by "nothing more than the agreement of the parties," and it "required neither witnesses nor written documents nor notification of authorities." The koinonia "operated when partners agreed to use property or labor in common towards a particular goal that was beyond the property or labor itself."[3]

The members of the koinonia viewed one another as partners who were mutually committed. Each person in the koinonia contributed to the koinonia as she or he had resource or ability. One person might commit labor, another money, another property. All gifts were honored as necessary to the koinonia, and all persons shared in gains or losses. The koinonia had the moral prerogative to call upon its individual members to adjust their contributions or behaviors so as to enhance the goals of the community. One member of the koinonia could represent the whole. The whole was represented in the life of the one. The koinonia was based on "mutual trust and reciprocity."[4] The participants in a koinonia were conjoined. In the limited sphere of the koinonia, they embodied the social ideal of the philosophers.

Philo was a learned Jewish scholar in Alexandria at the time of Jesus who engaged in mutual interpretation between Jewish and Hellenistic spheres of thought. He sought to show how Jewish tradition interpreted Hellenistic categories, and vice versa. In the process, Philo used the *koinonia* word family to speak of both the human relationship with God and the relationship of human beings with one another in the religious community. Philo called particular attention to koinonia with God through a sacral meal. Philo and Josephus look with favor upon the Essenes because the common life of Essenes represents the ideal mode of human community.[5]

The early Christian uses of koinonia resonate with this background. Paul explicitly understands the church as a koinonia. For instance, the apostle describes the Corinthians as called into the koinonia (NRSV: fellowship) of Christ (1 Corinthians 1:9). Paul's counsel to the Corinthian congregation assumes that the church is bonded as a koinonia. By virtue of being in koinonia with Paul, the Corinthians partake in the apostolic afflictions and in the apostolic consolation (2 Corinthians 1:7. The Lord's supper is a koinonial meal, and those who partake of it become partners with Christ (1 Corinthians 10:16–18). Paul blesses the community with the koinonia (NRSV: communion) of the Holy Spirit (2 Corinthians 13:13).

Paul thanks the Philippians for their koinonia (NRSV: sharing) in the gospel (Philippians 1:5). The Philippians have koinonia (sharing) in the Spirit (2:1). In fact, Paul draws upon language familiar to those in a koinonia when he urges the Philippians to "be of the same mind" (2:2) in their partnership with Paul, a partnership that is defined by the self-emptying of Jesus for the sake of the world (2:5–11). The Philippians are to exemplify that quality of koinonia in their common life. Paul's suffering for the gospel is koinonia (sharing) with the suffering of Jesus (3:10). In the Philippian partnership with Paul, the apostle provides missionary witness while the congregation provides financial support for the mission. In fact, Philippians 4:10–19 is the ancient equivalent of a "receipt" acknowledging that Paul has received the Philippian funds. The Macedonians are so eager to become a part of the gospel koinonia that they support Paul financially even though they are impoverished (2 Corinthians 8:4; cf. 9:13)[6.]

In the letter to the Romans, Paul makes it clear that the offering for the saints in Jerusalem is an act of koinonia. The offering is a particularly potent demonstration of koinonia, for it demonstrates the bondedness of Gentile Christian and Christian Jew. The Gentiles of Macedonia and Achaia "were pleased to do this." Indeed, the Gentiles owe such koinonia to the Jerusalem church, "for if the Gentiles have come to share in their spiritual blessings, they ought also to be of service to them in material things" (Romans 15:27). Koinonia transcends traditional human separations. Indeed, in a passage reminiscent of the Hebrew Bible's concern for those outside the community, the apostle admonishes the readers of Romans to extend koinonia to strangers (Romans 12:13).

Paul prays that the koinonia (NRSV: sharing) of Philemon's faith will be effective in the good that Philemon does for Christ (Philemon 6). Indeed, Paul exhorts Philemon as the apostle's partner (*koinonos*) to welcome Onesimus as if the slave were Paul.

We can see with particular force the practical outcome of the church as koinonia in Galatians 2. A dispute arose in the early church regarding the validity of Paul's Gentile mission. Galatians 2 describes the Jerusalem conference in which the leaders of the Jerusalem church and Paul come to an agreement as to how to understand the gospel mission and to divide responsibility for it. The church has a single mission, but as a result of the conference, it will henceforth have two faces: "When James and Cephas and John, who were acknowledged pillars, recognized the grace that had been given to me, they gave to Barnabas and me the right hand of fellowship, agreeing that we should go to the Gentiles and they to the circumcised" (Galatians 2:9). In a formal koinonia, the right hand was often used to seal an agreement.

Paul also understands the danger of having koinonia with the forces of malevolence. Paul exhorts the Corinthians not to partake of food that has been offered to idols because in so doing the Corinthians become partners (*koinonoi*) with demons (1 Corinthians 10:20). Cautioning the believers not to be mismatched with unbelievers, the apostle asks, "For what *koinonia* [NRSV: partnership] is there between righteousness and lawlessness?" (2 Corinthians 6:14).

According to the Lukan memory, koinonia characterized the life of the earliest Christian church. In the famous summary in Acts 2:42, "They devoted themselves to the apostles' teaching and fellowship [koinonia], to the breaking of bread and the prayers."While koinonia here could refer in a general way to close companionship, it seems likely to us that it evokes the more developed notion of koinonia articulated above. For Luke invokes the memory of the communal ideal when he says, "All who believed were together and had all things in common" (Acts 2:44).The early Christians put their possessions in the service of providing for the needs of the members of the community.The same theme is underlined in Acts 4:32–37. The importance of participating fully and materially in the koinonia is stressed by the fate of Ananias and Sapphira (Acts 5:1–10).

While the Fourth Gospel does not use the koinonia word family, the Johannine Jesus invokes the koinonia motif when he describes the disciples as "friends" (John 15:15). Jesus infuses the koinonia with power so that the koinonia is able to continue his ministry, and even magnify it, after his departure (John 14:12). In a similar vein, the Johannine letters understand the church as a koinonia. John says, "We declare to you what we have seen and heard so that you also may have koinonia [NRSV: fellowship] with us; and truly our fellowship [koinonia] is with the Father and with his Son Jesus Christ"(1 John 1:3).The writer urges the church to let koinonia with God and Christ permeate the community. Otherwise, their koinonia is a lie.The writer of 2 John warns the church not to receive a false teacher. For when the community welcomes false teaching, they are joined in koinonia with the evil deeds of that person (2 John 11).

Ephesians summarizes the early Christian understanding of koinonia when it says, "We are members of one another" (Ephesians 4:25). The church is a body in which each part is vitally related to all other parts.

Theological Perspectives on Koinonia

Contemporary process philosophy and theology particularly emphasize the interrelatedness of the members of the body with one another. According to process thought, the various elements of the world are inherently related to one another. A community is made up of individuals who are internally related to one another. The individual members are not just externally related. In an external relationship, they would exist in the same space, but they would relate by bumping into one another. In an internal relationship, we are affected internally by others, and they are affected by us.[7] Catherine Keller describes an internal relationship by saying that the "other enters my experience," and "it enters as an influence upon me: it makes a difference, and so I am no longer quite the same. But influence, to be more precise, is not working *upon* me so much as *into* me; in-fluence is that which flows in. If the other flows into the self, then the other is immanent to the self, to the inside being of that self."[8] By definition, in the koinonia, we are not only bound together; we are deeply affected by one another such that what happens to one has an effect upon all.

God, of course, participates in the Christian koinonia. In fact, relationships in the Christian koinonia, when they are at their best, derive their character from God, whose character is creative and empathic love. "Empathy means 'feeling with'; it entails compassion and genuine understanding—standing under the other. It involves feeling with the feelings of the other person; rejoicing in her joys, grieving with his grief. Love in this sense means taking the other into account, letting the other make a difference to one."[9] As members of the Christian koinonia, we live in relationships of empathy with all others in the community, including God. God is affected by all that happens to us. God affects us. We are affected by one another. We affect one another. And not only we who are immediately present but the communion (koinonia) of saints.

The relationships in the optimum Christian community mediate the gospel to one another. Our relationships embody unconditional love and justice. However, we do not always respond to God and one another in an optimal way. "We take God's gifts and decide how to respond to them—creatively, courageously, and faithfully, or anxiously, foot-draggingly, and negatively." We can "resist the call forward by digging in our heels in resistance" to creative change. "Faith, after all, is openness to God's future, and each of us knows the difficulties of being so open."[10] The church needs always to be gauging the degree to which its koinonia is creative of a gospel community, or the degree to which it is frustrating the purposes of the gospel.

Furthermore, koinonia is not limited to the Christian community. William Robinson, a British theologian of an earlier generation, said that koinonia "is the hidden structure of reality."[11] The universe itself is a koinonia. "We, God, and everybody and everything else are caught up in a big Koinonial web."[12] Every element in the cosmos shares in koinonia, including nature.

The extent to which we are "members of one another" is vast. We are really related, not necessarily consciously, to everything that goes into the making of us. That includes a life-sustaining environment, a solar system (where would we be without the solar energy that is the source of all energy on earth?), a universe, and God who both transcends and is immanent in the universe. The blood that flows through our veins has its affinities with the sea waters from which we came.[13]

In the cosmic koinonia, we have the freedom to choose for or against the qualities of life and relationship for others and for ourselves. Because all things are internally related, our decisions—even our smallest ones— are important because they affect others, and their effect upon others returns to have an effect upon us. Indeed, "who we are and what we do matter ultimately because we make a difference to the One who is ultimate."[14]

If the universe is inherently a vast koinonia, what is the purpose of Christian koinonia? The koinonia of the church is to function as a light in the world, a model of the koinonia that God desires for all communities and all individuals in the cosmos. One problem with the universe is that aspects of its koinonia go sour. Relationships can become distorted. Manipulation, exploitation, and oppression can replace love, creativity, and empathy. Consequently, God calls the church to demonstrate the quality of life—characterized by unconditional love and justice—that should permeate all relationships in the universe. At its best, Christian koinonia is a light for the koinonial web that is the world.

Changing Patterns of Koinonia in the Emerging Church

From the perspective of scripture and theology, Christian koinonia is the powerful interconnectedness that joins Christians at the deepest levels in the gospel. In the koinonia of the church, we are partners with God and with other Christians in the life of the gospel. We are responsible with God for one another in the full range of Christian existence—spiritual, relational, material.

The church does not provide koinonia as much as it *is* koinonia. Koinonia is not a series of discrete groups and activities within the church, but is constitutive of the nature of the church. Koinonia is all that we are and all that we do. Nonetheless, Christian koinonia requires practical modes of expression through groups, events, behaviors, and attitudes. The church needs to provide structures and occasions whereby members can experience Christian koinonia such that they understand koinonia to make an everyday difference in their lives and such that they can make their own contributions to the koinonia. Insofar as possible, we need to know one another by name, to know one another's stories, to possess the skills to listen to one another and to know how (and when) to speak to one another. Our relationships need to mediate the gospel to one another, and we need to know how to reflect on our relationships to gauge the degree to which they are optimally helping us experience the gospel and the points at which qualities of the Christian common life ought to conform more closely to the gospel. We need gospel-shaped means of intervening in parts of the koinonia that are working against the gospel and that are in danger of fouling the whole web.

In the middle years of this century, the long-established churches implemented koinonia by gathering people who had a particular trait or common interest and by using that commonality as a port through which to experience the gospel. The congregation was often subdivided into groups that were designed to generate koinonia. For instance, many congregations had adult Sunday school classes that had business meetings, singing, and Bible study on Sunday morning, and dinners, parties, and other gatherings through the week. The class often had a recruiter who was responsible for inviting new members to the class. A "sunshine coordinator" was responsible for keeping track of the welfare of the members, alerting a telephone tree to share news and to request cards or other forms of help for those who were sick or had need. A service leader would locate service projects for the class. A few of these classes still thrive. For instance, the Kum-Dubbles Class of the Monte Vista Christian Church (Disciples of Christ) in Albuquerque, New Mexico, has been the primary experience of Christian community for that congregation's Builders for almost fifty years.

In the same generation, many denominations sponsored women's fellowship groups (usually called by names such as Christian Women's Fellowship, United Methodist Women, etc.) that divided the women of the congregation into small groups, often called circles. The circle would meet once a month for study and refreshments and, like the Sunday school classes mentioned above, would have a sunshine coordinator and a service leader. The circles would gather once a month for a general meeting of all fellowship groups. Literally millions of women found these groups to be lively centers of Christian koinonia. From the 1920s through the 1950s, the North American church had its most successful men's work in this century in the form of men's Bible classes.

Ron Allen's father was second tenor in the quartet that sang only for the Big Brothers Bible Class in the First Christian Church (Disciples of Christ) in Poplar Bluff, Missouri. The average attendance of the class was

300. They rented a movie theater next door to the church to accommodate the crowds. They broadcast their class sessions on the radio. The format was lecture, and the teachers (who rotated from week to week) included a judge, two attorneys, and a physician, all accomplished public speakers.

The principle on which these phenomena were based is still compelling; namely, that the church can gather people who have a common trait or interest and take that commonality as a starting point for gospel koinonia. However, the Christian community needs to envision fresh commonalities and groupings around which to gather people, even while maintaining aspects of the previous expressions of koinonia that continue to work well. Today's congregation needs to offer a plurality of modes of koinonia.

Congregations in the long-established churches should not ruthlessly stop the koinonia groups and events that flourished in the mid-century church and that continue, if vestigially, today. Those patterns still serve quite a few members in many congregations, particularly people in the World War II generation. As noted in the previous chapter, many in the Builders' generation have a strong institutional orientation and find Sunday school and women's groups of the kind just described to be significant sources of Christian nourishment. The Big Brothers Bible Class still holds forth every Sunday (sans quartet and radio program), with an average attendance of eight.

However, such groups can no longer be considered the norm. The brute fact is that significant numbers of Boomers and Gen 13ers, at least in the old-line denominations, do not find the patterns of koinonia represented by the institutional Sunday school class and women's circles to be meaningful. Boomers and Gen 13ers seek koinonia, but in different modes. A part of the call of the leadership in the Christian community is to help the senior generations to realize the importance of developing forms of koinonia that fit as well with the rising generations as the older models fit with the older generations.

Much of the koinonia in the church takes shape in circumstances that are not specifically designated as koinonia events. For instance, people who work together on a project (e.g., repairing the soffit outside the window in the church kitchen) often find that in their joint effort they develop a koinonial bond. Persons in study groups discover that a multiple agenda has come to birth in the group; the process of engaging the study material brings the members of the group into koinonial relationship with one another. Sponsoring a youth trip often brings previously unacquainted adults into close bonds of understanding and empathy. The church's leadership, then, needs to help people name and nurture koinonia wherever it is manifest in the Christian community. And all Christians need to be alerted to the possibilities for koinonia that inhere throughout the life of the church. Koinonia ought to be part of the life-system of the church.

Consistent with a theme that permeates this book, the church needs to have an experimental mind-set about these attempts. Some will succeed. Some will not. In these matters, Christian leadership needs to acknowledge that we are very much feeling our way to discover what works and what does not. And we need to realize that no formula will guarantee success from community to community.

Koinonia through Small Groups

When it comes to formal planning for events that are designed to encourage koinonia, small groups seem to be a mode through which many congregations have great success in embodying Christian community. Indeed, some congregations today establish persons to oversee small group life. Many people today are attracted to small groups that are intended to meet for only a few weeks (perhaps 6–8 weeks), while some people are comfortable with weekend retreats, and others with committing themselves for much longer periods of time. Congregational planners need to provide a kind of smorgasbord of koinonia experiences that focus on different subjects that take place for different lengths of time at different times and places, and that utilize multiple formats.

Planners need to identify groupings in the congregation that might come together on the basis of a common quality or interest. The potential members of such a group need to be listed. Of course, such a list should include all persons within the congregation who might be interested. But it should also include persons from beyond the congregation who might be drawn. The planners need to seek input from the potentially interested parties about the type of experience and the times of the day and week that would be appealing. When putting together an attractive program, the planners need to consider ways in which the event can have a good chance to mediate Christian values. People need to be invited. Frankly, congregations in the long-established churches frequently do a poor job in the invitational phase. Such congregations often do little more than put a notice in the church newsletter the week before such an event is to take place. The congregation needs to be much more creative and assertive (without being pushy or manipulative). For instance, a thorough recruiting program would include notices in the church newsletter, announcements on Sunday, and letters mailed to potential participants (all of these long in advance of the launch of the event). It should also include personal visits to those who might benefit from the program, and creative printed material—for example, tasteful and imaginative flyers. And persons who were invited but did not respond should be contacted to find out why they did not. What can the church learn from those who did not come?

It may be helpful for persons guiding koinonia ministries to systematically think through categories that might be used to organize small group experiences. The church can often listen to the people themselves: What would they find helpful and attractive? However, people are not always aware of their needs; consequently, the congregation sometimes needs to help the members of the community become aware of issues to which they need to give attention. For purposes of illustration, we list some potential foci for groups, drawn from sociological, psychological, or intellectual categories.

- Increasing numbers of people are interested in the life of the spirit. They respond to groups that introduce them to approaches to prayer, meditation, Bible study, drawing from the well of Christian authors, and practices in spirituality.

- Greater numbers of people than in the recent past are expressing overt interest in Christian doctrine. A series of classes on what Christians can believe about God, Christ, and the Holy Spirit can be a significant experience of koinonia as people wrestle together with matters of ultimate concern.

- Many persons seek support in the midst of particular struggles, such as the loss of a partner or child, divorce, living with disabilities, discovering a new sexual identity, relocation, loss of job, addiction, dealing with aging parents, and adoption.

- Persons of particular ages and orientations often seek companionship with one another. For instance, congregations can offer distinct koinonia experiences for singles and marrieds across the age spans: young adult, early middle age, late middle age, early seniors, middle seniors.

- Persons of particular life orientations are frequently strengthened by koinonia with persons of similar bent. For example: singles support groups, support groups for various sexual orientations, support groups for people who are married.

- The church has only begun to envision new ways for Christian women to relate to one another in the church in the new millennium. The church needs to find out from women at different stations in life where they need encouragement and support. The church might begin by exploring women's interest in issues of living in a culture and a church that still operate with patriarchal biases, in issues that women face in the workplace and in the home, in disparate vocational and home lives, in how women can relate to one another when the women's spectrum in the congregation ranges from liberated feminist to conventional submissive spouse, in single motherhood on limited incomes. Many women appear to be ready to read, study, and talk together.

- The church very much needs to imagine how Christian men might relate together in the coming world. A congregation might discover from men what they would find helpful and interesting. We know men who are eager to know what it means to be a Christian friend, husband, and father today. How do men deal with pressures and dynamics affecting men in today's culture? What are realistic and Christian aspirations for a male life? And what are male fears and appropriate Christian responses? How ought men respond to the evolving roles of men and women in the workplace and in the home? Would men in the congregation like to have opportunities to work together on improving the church building, the homes of members, the homes or businesses of persons in the wider community? In many congregations, men respond in fewer numbers and with less enthusiasm to such offerings than do women. Consequently, congregations need to be persistent and patient when developing men's ministries.

- Parents—single and married—often welcome help with their families. Children and young people are occasionally receptive to help with their family lives.

- A significant number of people like to read and discuss books or watch and discuss videos about contemporary issues on which Christians need to ruminate. One group that we know started as a four-week study of the spirituality of John Irving's *A Prayer for Owen Meany*. The subject matter was so interesting and the koinonia so rich that the group turned their study into a year-long immersion in the spirituality of several of Irving's novels.

- A fair number of people are attracted to mission projects and, especially, to mission trips. The mission projects are themselves expressions of koinonia with those who need the encouragement provided by the mission. But the common work (e.g., erecting a house, refurbishing a church) becomes a koinonia-building experience for those who are engaged in the project. Such projects have appeal across the age spectrum. The youth mission trip is an honored tradition in many congregations. But adults of all ages are also attracted to such efforts. And mission trips can become marvelous intergenerational experiences of Christian koinonia.

■ An individual minister, or even a ministerial staff, can no longer provide sufficient person-to-person pastoral care for a whole congregation. One-on-one pastoral care is a practical, and often vital, expression of koinonia. Today's church needs to provide resources in addition to the clergy for pastoral care. A congregation needs to train lay elders or similar leaders to make calls on those who are hospitalized, homebound, traumatized, or otherwise in need of direct personal koinonia. A congregation may find it helpful to divide the congregation into small care-groups, with each group having a leader who is trained in facilitating care. (Such a program of congregational care cannot be undertaken quickly or lightly. It requires extensive training for the group facilitators, and it calls for extensive monitoring by the congregation's leaders to make sure that the groups continue to function after an initial honeymoon start-up period.) Further, the congregation as a whole needs to be schooled to realize that pastoral care is a calling of each member in the community to care for one another.

■ Many congregations have success with athletic programs for different age groups. However, it is easy for such programs to lose contact with Christian consciousness. The game is not the thing. The game is a means to experience koinonia. Consequently, at a minimum, athletic events should be preceded and followed by devotional moments in which the participants recollect the ultimate purpose of the program and commit themselves to treat all players in terms of the Christian koinonia.

■ As a part of developing a plurality of koinonia experiences, we even suggest that the old-line churches try a mid-century style Sunday school class or fellowship circle for Boomers. While this style of koinonia does not appeal to a lot of Boomers, it does to some. Such groups flourish among Boomers, and even a few Gen 13ers, in some congregations, usually found on the evangelical end of the theological spectrum. The keys to the success of such groups seem to be these: (1) Week by week, their lessons provide meaningful interpretations of life from a Christian perspective. (2) The group actively recruits new members. Usually a sparkplug person works hard at inviting new persons to come and keeps track of those who are absent. (3) The members regard the group as a primary source of social life.

The best of such groups often share common characteristics. They provide solid content on the subject matter. The people in the group have opportunity to talk with one another in depth in an environment of trust and security. Frequently this conversation is tentative at first but becomes deeper and more honest as the group proves itself trustworthy.

It is crucial for congregational leaders to see that each small group experience specifically name the presence and functioning of the gospel. Otherwise, small groups—even those sponsored by the church—can easily forget their particular character and their particular mission. Even worse, participants can assume that Christian koinonia involves no transcendent perspective or participant. As a particularly banal example, we cite a congregation, located near a popular fly-fishing river, that sponsored a Wednesday night fly-tying workshop during Lent. The only connection between the gospel and the people who eagerly came to tie flies was the fact that the meetings took place in the church's multipurpose room. The event left at least one participant with the impression that Christianity has no more to offer the contemporary world than fly-fishing. And, as he said, "I would a lot rather spend my Sunday mornings in a sparkling brook with the water laughing around me than in a dim sanctuary and those sad, old songs."

Koinonia in Larger Group Settings

Koinonia is realized in larger ecclesial settings, as well. Church leaders should seek for the koinonia of larger group venues to mediate the gospel in thoughts, actions, and relationships. Big groups can also develop a sense of interconnectedness and solidarity. Indeed, a moment in even the largest gatherings of the church can develop a significant level of intimacy, interawareness, and bondedness. The koinonia of the large group is especially important to church members who resist participating in small groups. For them the koinonia of one-to-one relationships and of larger group settings form their primary experience of embodied Christian community. Pastors and others need to monitor the quality of the koinonia that takes place in gatherings of high numbers of people because it is easy for such gatherings.

How can the congregation encourage gospel koinonia in a setting involving lots of people? Perhaps the most important step is to teach the congregation (through sermons, articles in the newsletter, classes, and teaching moments in group life) about Christian koinonia and about the importance of manifesting it in all aspects of the church's life. In addition, planners of large-scale events can seek ways in each group setting to help people be aware of their connection to one another in Christian community. Large-scale occasions require conscientious attention to helping the congregation realize the koinonia that is possible. Without such attention koinonia can be minimized and can even take a negative turn, as with the person who says, "I'm just a statistic, just another notch on the preacher's Bible."

Common happenings create a shared sense of life and memory. Even when we do not talk personally with others who are present at an event, we have a degree of knowledge of one another and a body of shared experience. A few years ago, the General Assembly of the Christian Church (Disciples of Christ), meeting that year in Tulsa, Oklahoma, had a moment of intense shared pain. Although the auditorium was overflowing with more than 7,000 people, that moment created a deep sense of connection among many. Today, when one person who was present says the name "Tulsa" to another who was present, they sometimes feel a bond. Often the speaking of the name is accompanied by a soulful look that says, "I know the suffering that is in your heart. It is my suffering, too. We carry it together."

The service of worship, even when it involves hundreds of people, can regularly create a genuine experience of koinonia. People are together in the same space. By virtue of that fact alone, we affect one another, and we are affected by one another. Collective worship can evoke the sense of being a part of a great belonging. The service is an hour of shared experience; it becomes an hour of shared history. The simple fact of doing things together can generate a sense of union with one another. For instance, when we sing or speak together, each person's voice is woven together with the voices of other people. We are physically touched by the sound waves generated by those around us. The things that we say in the presence of one another in worship, and that we say to one another, can help us feel our interrelatedness. As we hear, speak, sing, see, touch, act, think, and feel together, a congregation creates a common memory out of which it can live. A story told in a sermon can become a piece of the collective experience of the community as the story touches the minds, hearts, and wills of the community. Some congregations find that their koinonia is strengthened by inviting people to speak aloud their prayer concerns. (A caution: this part of the service can easily get so long, or some of the concerns can become so trivial, that the congregation is distracted and eager to get to the next part of the service.) Many congregations pass the peace, or share a holy hug or a holy kiss, to help demonstrate koinonia. Later, when people are alone, they can draw upon the collective power that was present in the service of worship as a vital energy source. Even when we are by ourselves, the memory of an experience of koinonia can be sustaining and empowering.

A generation ago, members of a congregation tended to live near one another and to see one another on a day-to-day basis in the town or neighborhood. But today the members of congregations, especially in urban and suburban areas, are often scattered. Many of the members of the congregation see one another only on Sunday or when they make a trip to a church meeting. Our conscious participation in koinonia is enhanced when we know something about one another. Consequently, a congregation needs to provide occasions when people can be together to learn names, to discover one another as persons.

Congregations need to find a number of ways to help persons be aware of one another as persons. We are best able to express koinonia for one another when we know each other by name and when we know something of one another's history and current life situations and issues. In the narthex and sanctuary prior to worship, we recommend that the congregation no longer be instructed to whisper or to sit in silence during an extended prelude. Instead, the people should be encouraged to talk with one another. Acts of speaking and touching help build a sense of community among those who are gathering for worship. We frequently see older people make their way down the aisle and lay a hand on one person, and then another, and exchange a soulful look and a few words, renewing the koinonia among them. If silence is needed at the beginning of the service, the worship leader can formally call the congregation to order and invoke a few moments of silence. Many congregations issue name tags as a way of helping people associate names and faces. A coffee hour before or after worship can be more than an exercise in drinking coffee and munching slightly stale doughnut holes; it can allow people a few moments of face-to-face koinonia that they otherwise might not have.

Since the earliest known human history, eating together has created a common bond. In the ancient world, food supplies were more tenuous than they are today in the middle-class parts of North America. To share food was to share that which is necessary for life. To give some of my food to you was to say, "Your life is important to me. I give some of that which I need to provide for your life." While few middle-class North Americans worry about whether they will have enough food, the fact of eating together continues to have symbolic connotations. When we sit at table together, we feel a certain bond.

Taking advantage of this phenomenon, many congregations find that small group dinners in the homes of the members allow people to get to get to know one another in settings other than Sunday morning services or formal church meetings. Common meals, picnics, ice cream socials, and other forms of eating together also bring people together in table fellowship. When they work in soup kitchens and food pantries, many groups in churches discover that their own sense of bondedness increases, as well as their sense of solidarity with the hungry. Congregations can help such meals serve Christian koinonia by helping the congregation to become conscious of the nature of Christian koinonia and of how it should be expressed in each mode of relationship and community.

Business meetings (and other similar occasions in the life of the church) can also intensify or frustrate Christian koinonia. The officers of the congregation need to make it clear that the agenda of the business meeting is to help order the congregation's witness to the gospel in effective ways. A goal of church administration is to examine the theological content being commended or embodied in the congregation's life and the patterns of relationship that are typical in the congregation, and to see that they serve development of koinonia in the best way that they can in the congregation's situation. The business meeting itself should be an experience of Christian koinonia. Toward this end, the presiding officers, or the pastor, may need to intervene from time to time to point out how the participants need to understand a certain issue (or the way the issue is being discussed) from the perspective of koinonia. A discussion marked by name-calling, caricature, illogic, various forms of stupidity, and unprocessed hostility works against the emergence of koinonia. Or the issue may be in the process of being resolved in such a way that its resolution will damage the koinonia. Concerns about the budget, parliamentary rules, the property, committee reports—these all need to be evaluated from the standpoints of their appropriateness to the gospel, intelligibility, moral plausibility, fittingness to context, and the degree to which they will enhance the koinonia.

Koinonia and the Wider Church and World

Christian koinonia extends beyond the small-group bondings within a congregation and even beyond the congregation itself. A danger of using common qualities or interests as focal points for small groups is that people can get the functional impression that their group is the extent of the concern of Christian koinonia. In a candid moment, Ron once heard an active member of a young adult group say, "I'm not in the senior citizens group. I don't understand old people. And I really don't care much about what they do." While this attitude may be understandable, it is not appropriate to the Christian koinonia. A small group of like-minded people can be a significant experience of koinonia. But the very point of koinonia is that all Christians, are, by definition, related to one another. The higher our consciousness of those with whom we are related, the deeper our appreciation of our community with them, the more our own lives can be enriched, the more empathetic we can be, and the more we can contribute to the enrichment of the koinonia. It follows that congregational leaders should encourage small groups to remember and reflect on their connection to the congregational community.

Christian koinonia also involves the denomination and the worldwide Christian community. By definition, Christians are internally related to other congregations in the denominational family, and across the interracial, international, intercultural Christian world. In the biblical sense, we are partners in the common mission of the gospel with all other Christian communities. We are affected by what happens to them, and we affect what happens among them.

The church needs to help its members catch a vision of their relatedness with other Christians and with practical possibilities for demonstrating our connectedness. What can we each contribute to the koinonia of gospel witness? Pastors and others are called to help a congregation heighten its sense of partnership with others in the worldwide witness to the gospel. Through the koinonia, each congregation makes a contribution to the common witness.

For example, the church in a war-torn developing nation seeks to witness to God's love and justice. But Christians in that setting are distracted from making a witness by their need of blankets, clothing, food, and money. The church in a developed nation gathers these items and sends them. This act is not "charity." It is the church from the developed nation enacting its share in the worldwide Christian koinonia. The church from the developed nation may send some workers to the war-torn land to help witness to God's love for all and God's will for justice for all. But the primary gospel witness in the developing country will be made by the local church. In order to make its witness, that church needs warmth, clothing, food, and financial resources. The church in the ravaged land contributes bodily presence as its part of the witness. The church in the prosperous land contributes resources as its share in the partnership. Christian teachers need to help congregations understand themselves in koinonial relationships with Christians in the wider church.

We need to focus on an element in the koinonial understanding of the church that may make some of our readers uneasy. If we are joined with all Christians in koinonia, then we are not only in relationship with Christians whom (frankly) we like. We are also joined at a deep level with Christians from whom we are fundamentally different, and with whom we are uncomfortable, and even in conflict. This is particularly noticeable with respect to issues that divide the so-called (and unfortunately named) Christian left and Christian right. Association between these two groups (and others on the Christian spectrum) sometimes degenerates to the point that they deal with one another in caricature and name-calling. This is not fitting for a Christian koinonia that seeks to mediate unconditional love and justice.

To be sure, the koinonia will often be marked by disagreements among its members. Partners frequently think differently not only about practical strategies but about the nature and purpose of the mission. But in a framework in which we understand ourselves to be inherently conjoined, such disagreements ought to be the starting points for mutual conversation. What are the respective perspectives? What do they have in common? Where do they differ? What are the convincing and not-so-convincing points of each? One community's contribution to the koinonia eventually may be to say to another community, "Your understanding of this issue is fundamentally wrong." If the Christian family cannot resolve the dispute, then the differing households may need to make their own witnesses. We can treat one another with the respect that ought to be part of a koinonial relationship even as we critique each other's witnesses.

In addition, as noted earlier, koinonia is the structure of reality. We are joined in empathetic relationship with all other elements of the cosmos. "The *Koinonial* web is much larger than what we usually call the church," and a view of koinonia "adequate to it must include and transcend the church . . . The *Koinonial* reality is vast."[15] A part of being a light to the world is illuminating the interconnection of all bits and pieces of reality, and of helping those bits and pieces relate together in a koinonia of love, justice, and moral treatment.

> We must be stewards of God's promise to us in the gospel, stewards of God's promised future, *God's basileia*, stewards of those hopes which God has implanted in us, stewards of the past and its richness, including all those now-forgotten alternatives which were once God's new lures offered to pull God's people forwards, stewards of that divine freedom, that discontent that urges us to respond positively to God's promises. We must be stewards of

hope—the hope that nuclear holocaust can be averted, the hope
that ecological collapse can be eluded, the hope that farm land
can stop being destroyed, the hope that our cities can become
the city of God, the hope that blacks and whites can find a koinonia
that still eludes them, the hope that pluralism in our society and
world can become dialogue and compassion and cease waging
the war of each against all, the hope that the God-given capacity
of each person to be a self-directing, self-determining creator of
oneself, a person with dignity and freedom, be extended to persons of both genders.[16]

Christians and non-Christians contribute to the positive development of the cosmic koinonia with acts of love and justice. Contrariwise,
Christians and non-Christians can diminish the quality of the koinonia
through values, attitudes, and behaviors that diminish love and justice.

Just as the church needs practical means (e.g., small group ministries)
to embody koinonia within the Christian community, so the congregation needs practical strategies for heightening the congregation's consciousness of the cosmic koinonial web and of contributing to it. Again,
the most important factor is to educate the congregation into the nature
and extent of the universal koinonia. Preachers, worship leaders, and congregational educators need to help the congregation become familiar with
the global and interstellar koinonia and with the way it impinges on the
congregation's life.

In a recent Lent, one of our pastors found an extremely effective way
to do so. Early in Lent, he preached on the connection between the violence that killed Jesus and violence on the streets of Indianapolis. Each
Sunday in Lent, prior to the prayers of the people, the pastor would read
the names and addresses of persons killed by violence during the preced-
ing week in Indianapolis. Many of the deaths took place in the same
quadrant of the city as the congregation. A couple of people were shot to
death within blocks of the church building. The sermon set the stage.
Then, the simple reading of the names and addresses created a bond of
prayer and concern between the congregation and those whose lives were
rearranged by violence. Worship leaders and educators can think of any
number of similar ways of helping a congregation realize its part in the
universal web of life.

The church can also increase koinonial awareness by sponsoring events
in which members encounter persons and settings that differ from the
typical congregational profile and context. Cross-cultural experiences can

be a particularly effective means of conscientization into *koinonia*. Members of the congregation might participate with persons from another culture in a joint project. They might go to another setting on a mission. They might make a study trip to another culture. Cross-cultural experiences do not have to involve great expense or time away from home. Most European Americans would have an immensely enlarging cross-cultural experience if they would participate in an aspect of the life of an African American community, or an Asian American, or Hispanic, community. Indeed, a middle-class European American group might find it eye-opening to participate in the life of a poor European American community. In certain neighborhoods of Indianapolis inhabited largely by Appalachians, I feel as much as if I am in a strange land as when our family spent the summer in Zambia. Participants in cross-cultural encounters ought to reflect on how their experience enriches (or otherwise affects) their understanding of koinonia in order to bring their fresh awareness into sharpest focus.

A congregation can also sponsor visitors from other nations or cultures or settings into its life. We know of one congregation that had the imagination and financial resources to call an "international minister" to its staff. This clergyperson, from another culture, became a living embodiment of the community's connectedness with other arenas in the world.

We pause long enough to note that some in the congregation will not be enthusiastic about expanding their koinonial vision. This is understandable. The new and the unknown are always a little frightening, and the more so in a setting fraught with so many present and future uncertainties. Pastors will often need to be creative and patient in dealing with congregational resistance (that often manifests itself passively) against expanding their direct involvement in the cosmic koinonia. We have noticed certain characteristics in congregations that seem to have the most success in helping people take an interest in, and responsibility for, the world-wide koinonia. The pastors speak in positive terms in preaching and teaching about the possibilities of those involvements; they acknowledge the negative and even judgmental dimensions of our participation in the koinonia, but they do not threaten the congregation unduly. Laypeople are on the public forefront of conceiving, planning, recruiting for, and supporting congregational efforts. Indeed, a congregation seems especially touched when some of its members have a significant experience of expansive koinonia that they report personally to the community at large.

A further part of the church's mission is to help its members understand that wherever they are and whatever they do—in church or out—

their actions contribute to the universal koinonia. "The work a laywoman does, day by day, of preserving the structures of justice and liberty in the society is perhaps more important than any committee work she might do at the local church."[17] The Christian community needs to help people name and celebrate all acts of love and justice.

Conclusion

We close with a theological reprise. God is the senior partner in the koinonia. "God presides over the world," as Whitehead says, "with a tender care that nothing be lost." "God bestows on our fleeting days," as the Jewish prayer book says, "an abiding worth." Consequently, "our slightest acts of kindness and concern for others are included in God's feelings and rendered everlasting." This notion has a practical implication. "What we do matters. It is meaningful. It counts. God is not only the giver of every good and perfect gift; God is also the perfect receiver of all our good and imperfect gifts. That should give us enough ground and warrant, and enough freedom, to be good stewards of God's varied grace."[18] Nothing that Christians, or non-Christians, do in the service of the koinonia is insignificant or lost.

The church *is* changing. A different kind of church is emerging from the one that many of us know. The constant in the change and emergence is the God who is ever with us, the God who ever loves the world without reserve, and who endlessly seeks just relationships in the world. The church is called to join God in exploring fresh forms of ecclesial life (or in renewing old ones) so that the Christian koinonia truly can be a light in the world. God promises that nothing—not even failure—is ever lost. That should give us enough courage to be bold in imagination, in experimentation, in risk. And, if the last light should be turned out in the last congregation of the long-established denominations, we can still look to the future in hope. For God is never without a witness in any time or place. The koinonia goes on.

6

The Church as
Living Community

Throughout this book we have talked about four ways in which vital congregations live out their life together in Christ. Our overall assertion is that these four indicators of congregational vitality tend to rise and fall together. An intense teaching/learning community that is not engaged in service to "the least of these" is on a "head-trip" that does not manifest itself in active discipleship. A congregation heavily involved in service but too busy to sit still and worship or study soon loses its sense of Christian identity. A numerically growing congregation that is inattentive to teaching and practicing the Christian faith becomes a warm social club with a thin veneer of Christianity as its outward coating. A liturgically powerful congregation that neither seeks to understand matters more deeply nor to live them out more authentically becomes a lovely liturgical island surrounded by a sea of strangers, the poor and the lost, in whom it fails to see the needs of Christ.

First, a robust congregation takes responsibility for the *kerygmatic* task of the church: making the apostolic witness to Jesus Christ. All churches, in one way or another, are faced with the problem of numbers. Perhaps they are growing, at whatever pace that growth might take place. Or if they are in a situation in which growth is difficult or impossible, such as a small town or neighborhood that is overchurched or in economic and social straits, they may have found a way to stem the decline in numbers. But numerical growth without faithful Christian witness to the gospel of Jesus Christ will finally not be self-sustaining. For that growing community to become a community transformed unto newness of life by the gospel of Christ, the gospel must be well and heartily proclaimed.

By *kerygma* we do not only have in mind preaching. We are using *kerygma* to refer to all the ways in which the gospel of Jesus Christ is presented to the congregation, but primarily we have in mind two of them: the presentation of the gospel in preaching and its presentation in the service of worship. By kerygma in this chapter, we intend these two functions. We know that the gospel is presented in other ways as well, as in feeding the hungry, but we deal with that under *diakonia*, service or mission.

Dynamic congregations grow in understanding the Christian faith. They attend carefully to the responsibility of the church for *didache*—for teaching the Christian faith. Churches of this sort accept the fact that if they do not teach the Christian faith, no other institution will. They have come to grips with the fact that growth in wisdom and understanding on the part of the congregation does not happen by accident or osmosis. They find numerous, dynamic, creative ways to teach the Christian faith and engage members of the congregation at their growing edges. They also know that if the congregation is going to live by the story that it tells, then it must tell the story by which it intends to live. One of the things this means is that a self-governing congregation in which the members play important decision-making roles only "works," as a Christian organization, if those members understand the Christian faith.

Robust congregations flourish in their development as organizations, becoming more of a functional community the various parts of which cohere and serve commonly agreed upon aims and goals. The *koinonia* (companionship) of the church that both hears and studies the word of God is another dimension of potential growth that cannot be neglected if a congregation is to be either genuinely Christian or comparatively healthy. Koinonia cannot be reduced to the watered-down feeling of warmth common to any members of a social club or characteristic of the warm tolerance of a cocktail party. Koinonia has to do with the kind of community shared by those who are companions of Jesus Christ, the "people of the Way" who are committed followers of the pioneer of our faith. The word "companion" stems from two Latin words, *cum* (meaning "with") and *panis* (meaning "bread"). Jesus' companions, therefore, are those with whom he breaks bread in communion and whom he calls his "friends"

(John 15:15). We are given and called to be "friends" of Jesus Christ, who as God incarnate, is Friend of all. We who are friends of the Friend of all are also given and called to befriend one another.

That brings us to the commandment of Christ that we feed the hungry, clothe the naked, visit widows and orphans in their afflictions and tend to the needs of the "least of these." Although we take it up last, it is first in order of priority that a congregation grow in mission and service to the world. We are given and called to embody the love of Christ in action directed at relieving the pain, suffering, and hunger of the world, revitalizing a neighborhood, developing housing for the elderly, rehabbing the homes of poor people, educating young people, and so on. We make the Christian witness in words and deeds—words acted out as deeds and deeds interpreted by words. An important part of mission is global and organized through judicatories, denominations, and ecumenical agencies. That is critical, and an authentic congregation will be responsible for it. But equally critical and perhaps unrecognized in its importance is the role of the congregation in hands-on ministry with those in need.

We choose to call this task or dimension of the church *diakonia,* or service. Diakonia has come, by custom and usage, to refer to service within the congregation. However, it was not always so. In the early church, the function of deacons was to see to it that the poor among the saints and the widows had food for their tables (Acts 6:1–6). In Alexander Campbell's understanding of church order, the ministry of deacons was that they were to be "public servants of the church in all things pertaining to its internal and external relations." Their duties included taking "care of the Lord's table, the bishop's table [seeing to the needs of the full-time elders], and the table of the poor."[1]

All these—*kerygma, didache, koinonia,* and *diakonia*—are included in the mission or purpose of the church, which is to witness to the gospel of Jesus Christ for the benefit of the world and to the glory of God. The basic ways in which the church does this are by way of constituting itself as a community devoted to the way of life that God gives us and to which God calls us and, by doing so, to witness to an alternative to the death-dealing ways so characteristic of the social, economic, and cultural world in which we live.

Congregational Stories: The Church as Living Community

The proof of the pudding is in the eating, and the proof of a theory of congregational vitality is in candid conversations with people significantly involved in the lives of a variety of congregations. Here we provide reports on extensive conversations with several such folk. Each report is a thumbnail sketch of certain aspects of the congregation, along with an effort to determine the relative presence or absence of our four factors and their relation to the congregation's overall well-being. The congregations are real, their names fictitious.

We chose these congregations because they represent a wide spectrum of situations. Some are large, some quite small, some mid-sized. Some of their pastors are men, some women. They represent several denominations. Some are located in inner cities, some in small towns, some in suburbs. All of them are struggling in one way or another.

St. Humphrey's On the Edge of Battle

St. Humphrey's (to the best of our knowledge there has never been a St. Humphrey) is a congregation located halfway between downtown and suburbia, with part of its neighborhood including the inner-city ghetto and another part an upscale, historic neighborhood of mansions built by some of the early moneyed citizens of the city. Its membership, which is smaller than it used to be, remains at about one thousand members; but the decline seems to have stalled, and St. Humphrey's is a stable congregation in a difficult context.

Diakonia: St. Humphrey's is a strongly community-oriented congregation; its mission statement accentuates the importance of its service to its neighborhood, its city, and the wider needs of a hurting world. For over a decade it has run a neighborhood soup kitchen several days a week, serving soup and sandwiches to all who come. It is in the process of constructing a new building that will contain a community room to provide further opportunities for community ministry and facilities for ministry to the homeless. It is involved with other congregations, neighborhood organizations, and local businesses in the hard slogging process of neighborhood revitalization that empowers the poor instead of moving them elsewhere for the sake of development. In this regard it is involved in property rehabilitation in the neighborhood and in bringing neighborhood housing stock up to code.

Kerygma: Its pastor provides a steady diet of solid, profoundly biblical preaching that addresses significant issues in the light of the gospel. Seminary faculty members who are also members of St. Humphrey's report that the preaching is consistently strong, reflective, theologically acute, and that it addresses the "weightier matters of the law." About half of the congregation is present in worship on any given Sunday (a little over 500 of the 1,000 members).

Didache: Even more are involved in some form of weekly Christian education. The average number of persons involved in Christian education every week is almost 700, with about 330 of these being adults. This is a strikingly high amount of exposure to ongoing Christian education. St. Humphrey's has a long and well-established tradition of being quite active in adult learning. Sunday school classes, adult forums, and Sunday afternoon or weekday series on special topics indicate that a wide variety of opportunities for Christian education are presented. The special adult forums usually number about 150 participants. Various seminary faculty members are frequently recruited to conduct short-term series of classes. Recently, a complaint arose from some members of the congregation that not enough educational opportunities were being offered! The congregation manifests a yearning to deal with and understand hard issues.

One minister in the congregation commented that St. Humphrey's understood that the health of the congregation's program in Christian education is a barometer of its overall spiritual health. If the Sunday school is prospering, he said, that's a sign that the congregation will, too. And if the Sunday school is declining, that foretells a congregational decline.

Koinonia: St. Humphrey's is not a congregation without disagreement and conflict. Too many issues are dealt with and too much significant Christian education is going on for everything to be calm and serene. But it is a congregation that has learned how to talk about its disagreements, to talk about them as though the people talking to one another are Christian, and to discuss these matters in both the language and the spirit of Christian faith. They have learned, by and large, how to disagree.

St. Humphrey's is, by any analysis, a vigorous congregation. It is in no way lethargic with regard to understanding the Christian faith, engaging in service to human hurts and hopes, or forming itself as a community of witness and mission. Its decisions do not always please either its more liberal or its more conservative members. But it is an interesting test case: all four of our critical factors—*kerygma, didache, koinonia,* and *diakonia*— are strongly in place and the congregation is spiritually vibrant. As measured by the norms of the Christian faith, it is an authentically "successful" congregation.

St. Xample of Revitalized Downtown

St. Xample, a formerly big-steeple congregation, is located in the heart of downtown. Although the downtown area is revitalizing as a place of business and residence, St. Xample is one of the few congregations that remain there; the rest long ago having fled either to the suburbs or to the edges of the city. St. Xample has about 300 active members and "friends." The friends constitute about 50 in number, and some of them are on a track to joining the church. The reason why these friends are taking some time to become enfolded in the congregation's life is that they are people who have been wounded by previous congregations, many of them having suffered emotionally and religiously at the hands of fundamentalist preachers and/or congregations. The pastor of St. Xample is a woman who has the advantage of not looking or sounding like the preachers who have hurt these people.

The immediate neighborhood of the church is one in which the housing has been badly depleted for a long period of time. For a while most of the members drove into the city to participate in the congregation, and only about 3 percent of the congregation lived near the church building. Now, about 35 percent live nearby and the rest drive in, some from considerable distances.

The congregation is a highly diverse group of people. Now, on any given Sunday, about 45 percent of the gathered congregation consists of gays and lesbians. This group started attending the church shortly after the funeral for a person who had died of AIDS. The way the pastor handled the funeral, and the fact that she did not interpret AIDS and death from AIDS as punishment from God but instead proclaimed the gospel of God's unconditional love for all unworthy sinners, prompted the surge of interest in the congregation among gays and lesbians. Currently one Buddhist and one Mormon also participate in the life of the congregation, leading to some interesting questions of practical theology: Does one have to re-baptize a Mormon?

The membership of the congregation had been in a long-term decline but now seems to have bottomed out, to have rebounded a bit, and to be holding steady. To put it mildly, the congregation is in a place in which it cannot expect significant increases in numbers on the basis of location alone.

Kerygma: The pastor is a brilliant, theologically articulate preacher. She does an excellent job of correlating the gospel of Jesus Christ with contemporary issues and questions, helping people make sense of their lives in relation to God and of God in relation to their lives. The essential function of the church, which is to help people understand the world in which they live in the light of the Christian faith and to understand how to live in that world, is attended to with intelligence and energy. The Bible is theologically engaged, and texts are wrestled with and brought into conversation about the nature and meaning of the gospel and its relation to human hurts and hopes.

Didache: The congregation has a significant program of Christian education for all ages. The pastor herself actively teaches three days a week, on Saturday afternoon, Sunday morning, and Monday evening. Classes range from biblical study to literary discussion groups to wide-ranging theological reflection on a variety of issues. The Saturday afternoon class, "Fundamentalists Anonymous," attracts a significant number of participants, many of whom regard themselves as escapees from more conservative backgrounds. The class is intellectually active and inquisitive. Its members are unwilling, says the pastor, to be satisfied with "hearing the story." They want to know what the story means, to understand it: "They want some basic, foundational theology." About one-third of the congregation is significantly involved in Christian education in some form at least once a week.

Koinonia: How does a congregation composed of so much diversity—older members who remain loyal, gays and lesbians attracted by a nonjudgmental ministry, and recovering fundamentalists seeking to overcome what the pastor calls "churchaphobia"—manage to be one functional whole? How does it avoid being no more than a series of conflicting and competitive parts? The answer lies, at St. Xample, in the fact that heavy emphasis is put on affirming and forming the congregation's Christian identity. "The identity of the congregation," says its pastor, "is in its Christian faith." The congregation is given to understand that they are people who can understand themselves ultimately in terms of, and only in terms of, the gospel of Jesus Christ: that they are among those whom God graciously loves and that they are therefore those who are called, in turn, to love God with all their selves and their neighbors as themselves. "Any other ax to grind," comments the pastor, "is way down the ladder." One problem the congregation constantly has to deal with is the fact that it contains within its membership a lot of the walking wounded who have been victimized and are on the alert to find a victimizer. But the core leaders of the congregation have developed the critical capacity to analyze and understand the behavior of the various members of the congregation. This capacity resulted partly from their involvement in Christian education and partly from the practical experience of having to understand what was going on in the congregation.

Diakonia: St. Xample has a rather intense involvement in hands-on mission in its neighborhood. For several decades, it has run a thrift shop that makes available free and low-cost clothing. Its clientele includes homeless people and released prisoners. The latter are particularly in need of clothes suitable for wearing to job interviews and to work (in cases where jobs are found). The thrift shop, which accepts clothes that have been donated, turns a small profit that is plowed back into the mission of the congregation.

The congregation also runs a food pantry that is staffed by volunteers. It houses on its premises an Offender Aid and Restoration program that targets released prisoners as those whom it tries to help. Several members of the congregation work as volunteers in this program. The church building also provides space for an Exodus Refugee Resettlement program in which the congregation also actively participates. The executive of the program is a member of the congregation.

One of the great benefits to the congregation of these hands-on mission efforts is that members who are involved in them are constantly being educated about the society and economy in which they live. They become acquainted with how things look from the underside, from the point of view of "the least of these." Their imaginations are expanded, says their pastor, about the human situation, its complexity and ambiguity. All in all, about 50 different church members have some sort of volunteer outlet every week. These volunteers come from every age cohort of the congregation, from teenagers through older members.

Like St. Humphrey's, St. Xample is also a vigorous and lively congregation. Although it is only about one-third the size of St. Humphrey's, it bears a lively witness to the gospel and proves attractive to people seeking to understand the meaning of life, to find genuine community, and to be directly involved in making a positive difference to "the least of these." It, too, shows the positive correlation between the various factors that have to be in place if a robust congregation is to happen. All four factors—kerygma, didache, koinonia and diakonia—are strong and reinforce one another. The teaching/learning character of the community helps members understand the Christian faith not only theoretically but practically, with regard to how they treat one another and how they engage the world, and their involvement in mission helps them better understand the Christian faith. That the congregation is on the rebound from despair and dismay and finding new vitality amid circumstances that are not auspicious is testimony to the power of Christian faith to revitalize a congregation.

St. Felicity by the Auto Alarm Shop

St. Felicity by the Auto Alarm Shop is located in a transitional neighborhood. It is a congregation of about 275 participating members, 125 of whom are typically present at worship and about 75–80 of whom can be found in Sunday school on any given weekend. In the 1950s the congregation numbered about 900 and had to have two worship services on Sunday. The average age of the adults in the congregation is about 60. The congregation has grown older than its surrounding neighborhoods, of which it has two, one to its west and one to its east. An auto alarm shop near the church symbolizes the transitions that are taking place in the neighborhood.

On its west, the inner city is moving closer to the church building. This area has undergone a shift from a stable, blue-collar community to a locality characterized by a more transient populace, with high turnover rates. Whereas it was once filled with people who owned their homes, now it contains rental properties filled with people who move in and out quickly. At one time major automobile manufacturers employed large numbers of people who lived there but with plant closings and downsizings this is no longer the case. To its east lies a "best-buy" neighborhood for starter homes that attract young, first-time home buyers. The living quality and state of the housing stock is "a real mixture," with significant differences from one block to another.

Kerygma: Preaching and the quality of the worship service are the strongest feature of St. Felicity. The pastors, a ministerial couple, approach preaching in a way characteristic of those who take a correlational approach to theology. They seek to interrelate the meaning of the Christian faith with the deepest human issues facing members of the congregation. Helping the gospel to come alive to people (or, better, helping people to come alive to the gospel) by indicating how the loving grace of God is the reassuring and challenging word that needs to be heard and that speaks to all our circumstances and conditions is what the preachers try to do.

The worship service is done quite well. It is described as "vital" and is the object of considerable congregational concern and interest. The music is good, the choir excellent both with regard to the quality of music and the kind of fellowship it provides for its members. Ways are provided whereby the congregation participates creatively in worship both as to its planning and in their lively presence on Sunday morning. Its commitment to kerygma is a real strength of this congregation.

Koinonia: When we ask the question, To what extent is this congregation a well-functioning unit and not just a series of jostling and competing parts? the answer is more mixed. There are elements of the congregation that get along well with each other. A lot of caretaking occurs among the members. A good number manage to get to church on Sunday, for example, because others give them rides back and forth.

But some members of St. Felicity by the Auto Alarm Shop actively dislike each other, and the word "hate" even crept into the description of how they interact. Formally, they try to cooperate with each other, but it often does not work well. "It is very easy," said one, "to step on someone's toes." How to describe this dimension of the congregation's life was difficult. One commented that as a whole the church functions fairly well, but some groups outside the core leadership do not. Another said that the congregation does not function well as a whole, only the core leadership does. The congregation has a number of perennially unresolvable issues on which it cannot make a decision because to do so would alienate some faction. For over a decade they have needed to restructure their internal governing apparatus to take account of the smaller size of the congregation, but they have been unable to do so. When it comes to making a decision, the congregation is "frozen." And the greatest attendance at meetings occurs when the expectation is that there will be a fight.

Part of the congregation's troubles can be traced to a time when inappropriate behavior by a pastor damaged the congregation's ability to trust one another or to trust subsequent pastors. This problem seems to be subsiding, and one of the pastors was recently told, "Our congregation seems to be friendlier since you've been here." But this has taken a long time and still has a way to go.

Diakonia: As to hands-on involvement in mission to the hurts and hopes of the world, there is some, but not much. "A few highly involved people," said one pastor, "carry most of the load." The congregation runs a food pantry in the church building. Church members donate the food, and the church secretary does most of the work of the food pantry. There is also a rummage room that makes available clothing and a variety of household items. A group of laity in the congregation has taken ownership of the rummage room and, as a consequence, it has become a vital focus of the congregation's ministry.

A senior citizens' group meets in the church building once a week to eat lunch and play cards. Some participants are members of the congregation. A neighborhood crime watch group uses the building, as does a preschool that meets three days a week. The congregation is good at making its building available for nonprofit groups with a constructive purpose. Overall, its commitment to diakonia, like its koinonia, could and should be more intense than it is.

Didache: About 75–80 people a week are involved in Sunday school classes. There is also a Wednesday morning Bible study group and a youth group that meets weekly. "It is difficult to keep enough adult involvement," said one pastor, "to keep the youth groups alive." There are four adult Sunday school classes, two of which are vital. Three of these classes are averse to receiving any leadership or suggestions from the pastors. One class is described as "sophisticated, open, and full of people who like to challenge themselves to understand the Christian faith better." The rest seem not to like to move out of their comfort zones.

All in all, St. Felicity illustrates our point, although in a largely (but not totally) negative way: The vitality of a congregation's kerygma, koinonia, didache, and diakonia move up and/or down together. That preaching and worship are done well is not surprising because the pastors are talented and committed, and this is an area in which they can make a difference. But the koinonia of the congregation has been badly damaged. The lingering distrust of pastoral leadership deters the congregation from letting the pastors do one of the things they should be more prepared than anyone else to do, and that is to engage in the active teaching of the Christian faith. Lack of adequate understanding of the Christian faith and refusing to be stretched and challenged by it at least contributes to, if it does not totally cause, the lethargy in the congregation's diakonia and does not help it out of its shortcomings in its life together. Pain and distrust in the congregation echo in all the functions of the church.

What should the pastoral leadership do in this situation? Obviously, it should keep doing well all the things that are now going well. The distrust and alienation in the congregation need to be addressed. As to teaching the Christian faith, one possibility would be to try to start new classes and groups on Sunday morning or at whatever other time might be convenient. These classes should be formed from people not yet involved in the church's educational mission. From these classes, one could then try to generate new hands-on approaches to mission. The sermon, too, can play a major role in this regard, as well as "discipling," working one-on-one with members of the congregation.

St. Christine's in Older Burb

St. Christine's in Older Burb has been at its present location for about 30 years. It moved from a crowded location in the city to what was, at the time, an area of corn fields through which ran a major road. In the 1950s suburbs began to grow around it. Today it is well-located on a nice piece of property with adequate parking, good community visibility, and a steadily growing congregation. Its pastor informed us that we should not overlook the "dumb luck" factor in analyzing the well-being of churches. St. Christine's has had its share of "dumb luck," mostly good. Perhaps we should create a new theological category for dumb luck; in any case, it should be celebrated.

St. Christine's has about 300 active members, with about 200 in worship on a typical Sunday. It is a 100-year-old congregation, very much like a county-seat congregation. Seventy-five to eighty percent of its members grew up in county-seat churches where religion is a public function and the church is not the only glue that holds the society together.

St. Christine's partakes of this character and benefits from it. Its various small groups are task-oriented.

Kerygma: The pastor's approach to preaching is one that seeks to engage people's lives with the gospel. One could probably characterize it fairly as a sort of "relevant neo-Reformation" theological approach to preaching. The worship service is the strong focus of the congregation's unity; it is a unitive occasion that brings the congregation together. The hymns are intentionally chosen to appeal to all the major tastes in the congregation: one classical hymn, one evangelical hymn, one new (and singable) hymn every Sunday. The congregation is equally intent about lay participation in worship; it is not entirely clergy-led. Lay members of the congregation give some of the prayers and meditations; they make the announcements and read the scriptures. The youth groups take up the offering. The worship service involves the congregation actively instead of treating them as spectators.

Koinonia: The members of St. Christine's get along with each other rather well. "Mostly, they like each other," reports the pastor. Each of the congregational elders is given responsibility to care for the members in a particular geographical zone. There are ten such zones with which the elders make connections. This is one way the congregation takes care of itself. The small groups in the congregation are mostly task- and fellowship-oriented. The women's groups are committed to both study and active mission projects. Other groups gather around the music ministry of the church, its variety of sports teams that involve many young people in the neighborhood, or one or another planning committee. Overall, the congregation is a well-functioning whole, a mixed and diverse group of people who work well together.

Didache: Christian education in St. Christine's looks like this: There are three long-standing adult Sunday school classes that are basic to the adult Christian education program. Two other adult classes provide introductions to biblical study and to understanding the Christian faith. All in all, about 60 adults are involved in Sunday school classes. Some 30 young people are also regular Sunday school participants. The women's groups, which include about 60 women, are always intentionally involved in study. A weekday Bible study class numbers about 15. The adult summer forum, composed of lecture/discussion sessions led by various people including seminary faculty, run from about 25–35 people weekly. A significantly high percentage of the congregation is involved in Christian education.

Diakonia: About one-third of the congregation, according to the pastor's estimate, is involved in Christian service to the hurts of the world. The congregation provides a unified Christmas-shopping service, helping people get not only food but various basic necessities. They support a food pantry at a neighboring congregation. Numerous work trips are sponsored. Some recently went to Missouri to rebuild a home for a mother and three children after the Mississippi River flooded a couple of years ago, and the youth group takes work trips to Appalachia. The congregation recently settled its fourth refugee family in the last decade. The women's groups have four different service projects each year. The annual Crop Walk and contributions to Church World Service are well supported.

The various sports teams of St. Christine are part of its outreach to its community. Open to people of various ages and both genders, these teams include large numbers of people from the church's neighborhood. So large, in fact, that the pastor estimates that most people in the neighborhood have been through the building and on the grounds and have a friendly feeling toward the congregation.

The pastor of St. Christine's thinks that its growing edge has to do with becoming more ethnically diverse. He feels that the congregation is too homogeneous. At present it contains two African American and eight Asian American families. Otherwise it is composed of European American, middle-management, suburban folk.

Again, like some of the other congregations we have studied, St. Christine's shows, in an affirmative way, that the four factors critical to the life of a congregation—its kerygma, didache, koinonia, and diakonia—move up and down together. At St. Christine's, we can be thankful that they are on the upswing.

St. Dubious on the Old Town Square

Another congregation that we studied began its life about forty years ago in a small town. The members were predominantly lower-middle-class working people with a sprinkling of school teachers included in the congregation. Over time, the small town became a prosperous bedroom community near a large city, and the populace filled up with business executives and professionals (lawyers, doctors). The congregation's mix of people changed correspondingly and grew until the newcomers became decision-makers in the congregation. Then a backlash occurred, and the older members began to actively drive away the newer. Overt church conflicts, hostility, and finding ways to undermine communally made decisions characterized and still characterize much of the life of St. Dubious on the Old Town Square.

Today the congregation has about 180 active members, about 90 of whom are typically in church and about 100 of whom are in some form of Christian education every week. There is a comparatively small, core group of older members and a larger group of newer ones whom the pastor has worked quite hard to bring into the congregation and to retain. Retaining them requires lots of work, pastoral care and attention, and organization into small fellowship groups that provide protection from the attacks of the older members.

Koinonia: "If this congregation does not survive," says the pastor, "it will be because of lack of koinonia within the congregation." The companionship among the newer members is good, but neither they nor the older members have many links with one another. The negative dynamics in the congregation seem to revolve around issues of control that motivate the older members in their concern to hang on to the levers of power. Such koinonia as the congregation has occurs in small groups, in missional and educational projects, and in worship.

Kerygma: The pastor is regarded as a fine and talented preacher, particularly by colleagues who have attended St. Dubious. The approach taken to preaching is that of the esteemed homiletics professor Fred Craddock: "inductive preaching." The pastor also reports benefiting from frequent reading of Calvin's commentaries on the Bible and says that much preaching has to do with correlating the majesty of God's grace with the misery of human sinfulness and evil. The congregation has the latter in abundance and needs to hear the former.

Worship in St. Dubious is quite well done. The music program has been significantly upgraded in its quality, as has the organ. All parts of the congregation participate actively in worship, including the young people. Recently they wrote the Christmas play after having read the birth narratives in Matthew and Luke. When a young person participates in a piano recital, she plays the piece in the worship service. Many of the prayers are given by members of the congregation. The pastor works hard at getting people involved in worship. Regularly she preaches a series of sermons on questions that the members would like to hear discussed. Many of these have to do with issues of biblical interpretation and with living one's life as a Christian in the world. Lots of education is intentionally done in the sermon, much of it quite basic.

Didache: A large percentage of the congregation (100 of the 180 active members) are involved regularly in some form of Christian education. There are a number of small groups doing Bible study, one older Sunday school class of long-standing, and one class of women. The congregation has used the "Disciple Bible Study" program, created by The United Methodist Church, and the "People of the Covenant" program, created by the Christian Church (Disciples of Christ), that is open to all age ranges of the church. Denominational study materials are used for the young people. In addition, the pastor has the young people working on a moral value every month. They discuss it, play a game that deals with it, and watch a movie that coordinates with it. Sometimes the worship service features a lay speaker dealing with it and has responses from members of the congregation discussing it, with the pastor providing a short theological wrap-up to the service. Also, a lot of mission education goes on.

"Everything," comments the pastor, "ties into worship." The educational process feeds into the worship service, and prayer groups participate in the worship service, as do the book-studies groups, which are also prayer and discussion groups. Also, the congregation does a lot of educational work with lunches, sponsoring programs on various topics with outside speakers, arranged according to the interests and questions of the groups. It participates in the Walk to Emmaus retreat for training Christian leaders. The pastor has worked hard in board meetings at getting the board of the church to talk the language of the Christian faith and to speak to one another in ways appropriate to the Christian faith. Obviously, St. Dubious's pastor, who spark-plugs the worship and educational life of the congregation, provides significant opportunities for Christian growth for the congregation.

Diakonia: The congregation's participation in mission is also strong. The pastor places a strong emphasis on tithing, with the result that a number of the members tithe, and the congregation itself gives one-tenth of its income to outreach causes. The larger part of this outreach money goes for general causes for which the denomination is responsible, and another part goes for local causes as decided by the outreach committee. Another part is given to the young people to decide what shall be done with it.

A lot of hands-on mission projects are undertaken. The congregation participates in Habitat for Humanity, works at a care center for the homeless doing such jobs as painting, and some of the medical personnel in the congregation participate in health fairs or work at a center providing health care for homeless people. The congregation collects food for a center for people suffering with HIV. These involvements are celebrated in the worship service, offered to God as part of the congregation's gift, and the food collected for the HIV center is blessed in the worship service. The congregation is an active participant in the CROP walk, in which it raises a lot of money. It provides tutoring for young people facing difficulties and for Japanese women in the English language. It is starting a series on how to provide home health care for ill people who are homebound.

St. Dubious presents something of the same dilemma we have seen in some of the other congregations we have looked at—the quality of its common life (koinonia) is little short of ghastly and has by and large successfully defied all efforts to improve it. It is the one negative feature of this congregation's life. The other factors (kerygma, didache, and diakonia) are all quite positive. Of course, were it not for the negativity in the congregation's common life its numbers could be considerably healthier. The pastor and I discussed what could be done about its koinonia and agreed that a new approach to intercessory prayer might be helpful. That is, we came up with the idea of instituting a regular program that would get the older and younger members actively praying for one another and would also encourage them to do something positive in relation to each other in addition to praying.

St. William in the Woods

St. William in the Woods is a rural congregation. Larger congregations of the same and similar denominations, offering many more services to people looking for a church, abound in a county seat about ten miles away. St. William's is also near a locally well-known resort area. Slightly less than 150 members participate in St. William's, about half of whom do so on a regular basis. Typical Sunday attendance is between 40 and 50, and the congregation's budget does not support a wide array of programs. Because families looking for Sunday school classes and programs for their children drive into the county seat, St. William's is described by its pastor as a "gray-headed congregation with very few young families with children."

One of the real problems it faces is that too many of its older members are unable or unwilling to take upon themselves the tasks that need to be done if the congregation is avoid becoming what its pastor calls "an old-age home for Christians." Some of the older members are "snow birds" who fly south for the winter. Others simply say that they've done their stints at working for the church, and now it's time for someone else to shoulder the load. The problem is that there are few others to do so.

As to koinonia, St. William's is a congregation that gets along with itself quite well. It is devoid of power struggles and cliques. The quality of its internal life, says its pastor, is "great, with people who are very dedicated and deeply committed to the Christian life." This quality results from careful attention to relationships in the congregation.

Because of the size of the congregation, it long served as a teaching congregation for seminary students who were, in effect, doing internships in ministry. With frequent turnover in its leadership, it never developed much continuity of programming, a lack that the current minister is seeking to correct. Congregational members are responding well to the possibility of thinking long-range about ways to strengthen their congregational life.

As to the teaching (didache) of the Christian faith in the congregation, the pastor provides year-long studies of the scriptures (one year in each testament). Bible study classes take place on weekdays, with the regular Sunday school classes on Sunday. The classes for older people are strong in attendance, quality of discussion, and mission and social activities outside of Sunday morning. The classes for younger adults and children are more sparsely attended because families with children tend to drive the ten extra minutes into the county seat to participate in church. The pastor points out that the nearby farms can no longer sustain multiple generations of families, and that many farmhouses have been sold to people who use them for weekend retreats.

The congregation is particularly strong in service (diakonia). The members carry on a number of local mission projects through which they express God's love for the world and God's call for justice for all. These projects include "blanket Sunday," helping out in the local nursing homes, support of the church's food pantry, and staffing the community's crisis intervention center. Given its small numbers, the congregation has a vigorous social presence.

The kerygma at St. William's is characterized by preaching that alternates between teaching sermons (that give much attention to reflective study of the Bible with application to daily life) and sermons that announce the gospel. The worship service is fairly typical of those in the long-established Protestant denominations and in the congregation's denominational tradition.

St. William in the Woods is a congregation that can be said to be vibrant in its diakonia, kerygma, and didache for older adults. But it is also a congregation in danger of disappearing. For a congregation to decide to close its ministry can be a faithful and responsible decision. But it is also clear that a greater energy on the part of some members to provide ministries, such as Christian education for families with children, could meet an immediate need. The success of the congregation in its mission outreach shows that the members have plenty of energy and creativity. Perhaps St. William in the Woods could adopt the "Field of Dreams" approach to Christian education: "Build it, and they will come." Such an approach has worked, and not only in the movies.

Conclusion

This series of congregational snapshots gives us reason to believe that the overall claim we are making seems to hold true. The four crucial measures of a congregation's health and the four aspects essential to its Christian identity as the people of God—its *kerygma, didache, koinonia,* and *diakonia*—tend to rise and fall together. Each factor is critical and needs the attention of pastoral leadership if it is to develop well in a congregation. In this chapter, our focus has primarily been on the role of diakonia, understood both as hands-on ministry to the needs of a hurting world and as the more general outreach that a congregation effects through denominational and ecumenical service agencies.

Our claim is both normative and descriptive. The normative claim is that no congregation may properly claim the name "Christian" unless it actively engages in extending the ministry of Jesus Christ to the poor and those in need (of whatever kind). The more descriptive claim is that this kind of engagement, particularly the hands-on kind, contributes to the health and vigor of a congregation. It is also, as one pastor noted, a part of the educational program of the congregation. Members who work in soup kitchens or thrift shops, for example, either already know or learn more about the world in which they live than those who do not.

In order to help the congregation become a functioning whole manifesting genuine koinonia, we suggest some simple steps. One is that the congregation's annual budget should not be what it so typically is: a money-only budget laid out in two columns representing anticipated income and expenses. Since when we talk about stewardship we hardly restrict ourselves to the topic of money, why does the budget seem to contradict our talk? Why should there not also be a "budget" for time and talent, in which the nonmonetary contributions of members are celebrated and the ministry of the church spelled out?

Second, we learned from one pastor who commented above that in her congregation, "everything focuses on the worship service." This is a wonderful way both to offer to God, in the offertory, more than money and (in some churches) bread and wine. What would it mean for a congregation to celebrate in its worship the offering to God of its ministry to youth, to troubled teenagers, to those with learning disabilities, to the homeless, to inner-city kids struggling with growing up in a hostile environment, to widows trying to discover how to live in a new and recently desolated time of life? It should also celebrate and offer to God all its efforts at teaching and learning the Christian faith, as well as its common life together in Christ.

Third, in studying these and other congregations, we learned that the congregations that function most healthily with regard to koinonia are also congregations that have a higher percentage of adults involved in various forms of serious theological learning. There are many reasons for strengthening the teaching role of the minister and of other members of the congregation, and we spell these out in our chapter on teaching. But one seems to be that the more people learn how to talk with one another about the meaning of the Christian faith, the more they are able to talk with one another about how the congregation should go about living out the Christian faith. A major problem in mainline congregations, in other words, is getting past the fear of conversation about important matters. Genuine conversation is the friend of congregational vitality, not its enemy.

If all these aspects of the life of the people of God are celebrated and rendered important in worship, that helps to create a unified community of faith. If all these other things are consistently omitted from attention in worship, that, too, teaches something. It teaches that what is really important is this one hour a week, and everything else somewhat less so. A vibrant congregation celebrates all aspects of the life that God gives it as gracious gifts graciously to be shared.

Notes

Introduction

[1] See William Strauss and Neil Howe, *Generations: The History of America's Future* (New York: William Morrow, 1991), pp. 284–85.

[2] Note similarly Loren B. Mead, *Transforming Congregations for the Future. Once and Future Church Series* (Washington, D.C.: The Alban Institute, 1994), pp. 43–71.

Chapter One: The Congregation: Ideal Images, Harsh Realities, and Exhilarating Visions

[1] Walter Brueggemann, *A Social Reading of the Old Testament*, ed. Patrick D. Miller (Minneapolis: Fortress Press, 1994), p. 18.

[2] Ibid., pp. 43–54.

[3] This portrait of Jesus is indebted to John Dominic Crossan, *The Historical Jesus: The Life of a Mediterranean Jewish Peasant* (San Francisco: HarperSanFrancisco, 1991), esp. pp. 265–302.

[4] For an excellent study of varieties in the earliest churches, see Paul Minear, *Images of the Church in the New Testament* (Philadelphia: Westminster, 1960).

[5] Paul Tillich, *Systematic Theology* (Chicago: University of Chicago Press, 1963), vol. 3, p. 167.

[6] Robert L. Wilken, *The Myth of Christian Beginnings* (Garden City, New York: Doubleday, 1971), p. 158.

[7] See Norman Perrin, *The New Testament: An Introduction* (New York: Harcourt, Brace, Jovanovich, 1974), pp. 50–51.

[8] Minear, *Images of the Church*, pp. 33–34.

[9] William McKinney and Wade Clark Roof, *American Mainline Religion* (New Brunswick, New Jersey: Rutgers University Press, 1987), p. 16.

[10] See Loren Mead, *More Than Numbers* (Washington, D.C.: The Alban Institute, 1993), p. 37.

[11] Kennon L. Callahan, *Effective Church Leadership* (San Francisco: HarperSanFrancisco, 1990), p. 3.

[12] Ibid., p. 4.

[13] Ibid., p. 20.

[14] Stanley Hauerwas and William H. Willimon, *Resident Aliens* (Nashville: Abingdon, 1989), pp. 17, 16, respectively.

[15] E. S. Ames, *The New Orthodoxy* (Chicago: University of Chicago Press, 1918), p. 12.

[16] See Brueggemann, *Social Reading of the Old Testament*, pp. 265–266. The ensuing discussion of paradigms of the religious community in the Hebrew Bible is indebted to Brueggemann's incisive analysis.

[17] Ibid., pp. 267–268.

[18] Ibid., pp. 269–272.

[19] See our description of teaching in the life of the early church in Clark M. Williamson and Ronald J. Allen, *The Teaching Minister* (Louisville: Westminster/John Knox, 1991), pp. 35–46.

Chapter Two: The Vocation of the Church: Light of the World

[1] The notion of continuity and change is borrowed from Mary Elizabeth Moore, *Education for Continuity and Change* (Nashville: Abingdon, 1983).

[2] We state only one way of understanding the church. For other approaches, see Avery Dulles, *Models of the Church* (New York: Doubleday, 1974).

[3] Clark M. Williamson, *A Guest in the House of Israel: Post-Holocaust Church Theology* (Louisville: Westminster/John Knox, 1993), p. 248.

[4] See John W. Rogerson, "The Hebrew Conception of Corporate Personality," in *Anthropological Approaches to the Old Testament*, ed. Bernhard Lang (Philadelphia: Fortress, 1985), pp. 43–59.

[5] On the relationship between individual and community, see Clark M. Williamson and Ronald J. Allen, *A Credible and Timely Word* (St. Louis: Chalice Press, 1991), pp. 5–6, and Catherine Keller, *From a Broken Web* (Boston: Beacon, 1986).

[6] This formulation of the gospel is further explored in many of our writings, e.g., Clark M. Williamson, "Preaching the Gospel: Some Theological Reflections," *Encounter* 49 (1989): p. 191; Clark M. Williamson and Ronald J. Allen, *Interpreting Difficult Texts: Anti-Judaism and Christian Preaching* (Philadelphia: Trinity Press International and London: SCM, 1989), pp. 6–8, 60–72; idem, *Teaching Minister*, pp. 75–82; idem, *Credible and Timely Word*, pp. 71–88.

[7] We are aware of difficulties in the use of the terms "light" and "darkness" as figures of speech in religious discourse. See Ronald J. Allen, "The Language of Color in the Service of Justice," *Quarterly Review* 12/3 (1992): 17–26.

[8] For convenient surveys, see Hans Conzelmann, "*phos*," in *Theological Dictionary of the New Testament*, ed. Gerhard Friedrich Kittel, trans. Geoffrey Bromiley (Grand Rapids, Michigan: Eerdmans, 1974), vol. 9, pp. 310–358.

[9] On mutual critical correlation, see David Tracy, *Blessed Rage for Order: The New Pluralism in Theology* (New York: Seabury, 1975); idem, *The Analogical Imagination: Christian Theology and the Culture of Pluralism* (New York: Crossroad, 1981); idem, "Theological Method," in *Christian Theology: An Introduction to Its Traditions and Tasks, Revised and Enlarged*, ed. Peter C. Hodgson and Robert H. King (Philadelphia: Fortress, 1985), pp. 35–60, esp. pp. 52–59; idem, "Hermeneutical Reflections in the New Paradigm," in *Paradigm Change in Theology*, ed. Hans Kueng and David Tracy, trans. Margaret Koehl (Edinburgh: T & T Clark, 1989), pp. 334–362.

[10] We say "some" technologies because not all are appropriate for the church's use. For criteria of assessment, see the next subsection.

[11] These are developed in Williamson and Allen, *Interpreting Difficult Texts*, pp. 56–72; idem, *Credible and Timely Word*, pp. 71–79, 101–111; idem, *Teaching Minister*, pp. 75–82.

[12] On the "fittingness" of theological witness to particular contexts, see Schubert Ogden, "The Service of Theology to the Servant Task of Ministry," in *The Pastor as Servant*, ed. Earl E. Shelp and Ronald H. Sunderland (New York: Pilgrim, 1986), p. 88ff.

[13] For an exploration of the meanings of postmodernism, see Ronald J. Allen, Barbara Shires Blaisdell, and Scott Black Johnston, *Theology for Preaching: Authority, Truth, and Knowledge of God in a Postmodern Ethos* (Nashville: Abingdon, 1997).

[14] Leander Keck, *The Church Confident* (Nashville: Abingdon, 1993), pp. 27–33, 38–42.

[15] Craig Dykstra, *Growing the Christian Life* (Louisville: PCUSA, 1993), pp. 27–28.

Chapter Three: An Intense Teaching and Learning Community

[1] Loren B. Mead, *More Than Numbers* (Washington, D.C.: The Alban Institute, 1993), p. 36.

[2] Ibid., p. 37.

[3] Ibid.

[4] Ibid., p. 13.

[5] William Chris Hobgood and Ann Updegraff-Spleth, *The Congregation: Sign of Hope* (St. Louis: Chalice, 1989), p. 16.

[6] Ibid., pp. 18–20.

[7] Ibid., pp. 20–23.

[8] Ibid., pp. 23–25.

[9] Stanley Hauerwas and William Willimon, *Resident Aliens* (Nashville: Abingdon, 1989), p. 18.

[10] Ibid.

[11] Ibid.

[12] John Calvin, *Institutes of the Christian Religion*, ed. J. T. McNeill, trans. by Ford Lewis Battles (Philadelphia: Westminster, 1960), vol. 2, p. 1054.

[13] Clark M. Williamson, *Has God Rejected His People?* (Nashville: Abingdon, 1982), p. 155.

[14] Langdon Gilkey, *How the Church Can Minister to the World Without Losing Itself* (New York: Harper & Row, 1964), p. 80.

[15] See Williamson and Allen, *Teaching Minister*, pp. 106–109.

[16] Wesner Fallaw, *Church Education for Tomorrow* (Philadelphia: Westminster, 1960).

[17] Ibid., p. 10.

[18] See Williamson and Allen, *Teaching Minister*, pp. 106–109.

[19] Ibid., p. 106.

[20] Ibid., p. 107.

[21] Loren B. Mead, *More than Numbers*, p. 44.

[22] Ibid.

[23] Ibid., p. 45.

Chapter Four: Worship and Preaching in the Emerging Church

[1] For our developed views on this topic, see Clark M. Williamson and Ronald J. Allen, *Adventures of the Spirit: A Guide to Worship from the Perspective of Process Theology* (Lanham, Maryland: University Press of America, 1997).

[2] Keith Watkins, et al., *Thankful Praise* (St. Louis: CBP Press, 1987), p. 24.

[3] For example, see Ronald J. Allen, *The Teaching Sermon* (Nashville: Abingdon, 1995).

[4] Susan J. White, *Christian Worship and Technological Change* (Nashville: Abingdon, 1994), p. 122.

[5] Ibid., p. 128.

[6] Ibid., pp. 89–106.

[7] Many preachers shaped by the mechanistic world view envisioned religion as a system of spiritual laws that could be applied to life for the benefit of the congregation. One of the preacher's purposes was to help the congregation correctly perceive how the laws of nature interacted with the laws of religion.

[8] Walter Ong, *The Presence of the Word* (New Haven: Yale University Press, 1967), pp. 17–110; idem, *Orality and Literacy* (Methuen, 1984).

9 Wade Clark Roof, *A Generation of Seekers* (San Francisco: HarperSanFrancisco, 1993).

10 Keith Watkins, "A Sunday in Louisville: Contrasting Modes of Cultural Accommodation in the Liturgy," *Encounter* 57 (1996): 37–50.

11 Ibid.

12 Henry H. Mitchell, *The Recovery of Preaching* (San Francisco: Harper and Row, 1977), p. 56.

13 For a description of one of the most famous approaches to ministry with seekers, see the videotape "An Inside Look at the Willow Creek Seeker Service" (Grand Rapids: Zondervan Video Resources, 1993).

Chapter Five: Christian Koinonia—More than Animal Warmth

1 For a concise history of *koinonia* see Friedrich Hauck, "*koinos*" in *Theological Dictionary of the New Testament,* ed. Gerhard Kittel, trans. Geoffrey W. Bromily (Grand Rapids, Michigan: Eerdmans, 1965), vol. 3, pp. 789–809.

2 Ibid., p. 794.

3 J. Paul Sampley, *Pauline Partnership in Christ* (Philadelphia: Fortress, 1980), p. 12.

4 Ibid., p. 14.

5 Hauck, p. 803.

6 See further, Ronald J. Allen, "Preaching about Stewardship: *Koinonia* and the Christian Relationship with Resources," in *Preaching In and Out of Season*, ed. Thomas G. Long and Neely D. McCarter (Louisvllle: Westminster/John Knox, 1990), pp. 104–117.

7 On internal and external relationships, see Alfred North Whitehead, *Process and Reality*, Corrected Edition, ed. David Ray Griffin and Donald W. Sherburne (New York: Free Press, 1978), pp. 58–59, 286–288, 307–309, 328.

8 Catherine Keller, *From a Broken Web* (Boston: Beacon, 1986), p. 27.

9 Clark M. Williamson, "Good Stewards of God's Varied Grace," *Encounter* 47 (1986): 77.

10 Ibid., pp. 78–79.

11 William Robinson, *The Biblical Doctrine of the Church* (St. Louis: Bethany, 1949), p. 15.

12 Williamson, "Good Stewards of God's Varied Grace," p. 77.

13 Ibid.

14 Ibid., p. 77.

15 Ibid., p. 79.

16 Ibid.

17 Ibid., p. 80.

18 Ibid., p. 81.

Chapter Six: The Church as Living Community

1 Alexander Campbell, "Order," *Millennial Harbinger Extra*, no. 8 (Bethany, Virginia, 1835), pp. 504–507.